1

Christ Our Life

God Is Good

AUTHORS

Sisters of Notre Dame of Chardon, Ohio

Sister Mary Theresa Betz, S.N.D.
Sister Mary Kathleen Glavich, S.N.D.
Sister Jeanne Mary Nieminen, S.N.D.

THEOLOGICAL ADVISOR

Sister Agnes Cunningham, S.S.C.M.

CONSULTANTS

The Reverend Edward H. Konerman, S.J.
The Reverend Monsignor Joseph T. Moriarty

GENERAL EDITOR

Sister Mary Kathleen Glavich, S.N.D.

LOYOLAPRESS.

CHICAGO

Nihil Obstat: The Reverend John G. Vrana, S.T.D., Censor Deputatus
Imprimatur: The Most Reverend Anthony M. Pilla, D.D., M.A., Bishop of Cleveland
Given at Cleveland, Ohio, on 5 March 1996

The *Nihil Obstat* and *Imprimatur* are official declarations that a book or pamphlet is free of doctrinal or moral error. No implication is contained therein that those who have granted the *Nihil Obstat* and *Imprimatur* agree with the contents, opinions, or statements expressed.

Christ Our Life
found to be in conformity

The Ad Hoc Committee to Oversee the Use of the Catechism, National Conference of Catholic Bishops, has found this catechetical series, copyright 1997 and 2002, to be in conformity with the *Catechism of the Catholic Church.*

Dedicated to St. Julie Billiart, foundress of the Sisters of Notre Dame, in gratitude for her inspiration and example

Acknowledgments

This present revision of the Christ Our Life series is the work of countless people. In particular, we acknowledge and thank the following for their roles in the project:

- The Sisters of Notre Dame who supported the production of the Christ Our Life series, especially Sister Mary Joell Overman, S.N.D.; Sister Mary Frances Murray, S.N.D.; and Sister Mary Margaret Hess, S.N.D.
- The Sisters of Notre Dame and others who over the past twenty years have shaped, written, and edited editions of the Christ Our Life series, in particular Sister Mary de Angelis Bothwell, S.N.D., the former editor
- Those who worked on different stages involved in producing this edition, especially Sister Mary Julie Boehnlein, S.N.D.; Sister Linda Marie Gecewicz, S.N.D.; Sister Mary Beth Gray, S.N.D.; Sister Joanmarie Harks, S.N.D.; Sister Rita Mary Harwood, S.N.D.; Sister Mary Nanette Herman, S.N.D.; Sister Mary Andrew Miller, S.N.D.; Sister Mary Catherine Rennecker, S.N.D.; and Sister Mary St. Jude Weisensell, S.N.D.
- Those catechists, directors of religious education, priests, parents, students, and others who responded to surveys, returned evaluation forms, wrote letters, or participated in interviews to help improve the series

Scripture selections are taken from *The New American Bible* copyright ©1991, 1986, 1970 by the Confraternity of Christian Doctrine, Washington, D.C., and are used by license of copyright owner. All rights reserved.

Excerpts from the English translation of *A Book of Prayers* © 1982, International Committee on English in the Liturgy, Inc. (ICEL); excerpts from the English translation of *Book of Blessings* © 1988, ICEL. All rights reserved.

English translation of *Gloria Patri* by the International Consultation on English Texts.

Excerpt from *John Paul II in America: Talks Given on the Papal Tour, September 1987* © 1988 by St. Paul Books and Media, 50 St. Paul's Avenue, Boston, MA 02130, is used by permission of the publisher.

All attempts possible have been made to contact the publisher for cited works in this book.

Photographs

© **John H. Anderson/Photographic Resources** (p. 99); © **Bettman/CORBIS** (p. 80); © **Peter Cade/Tony Stone Images** (p. 39); © **Cleo Freelance Photography** (pp. 31, 36); © **Corbis Corp.** (p. 25 top left); © **Corel Corporation** (p. 142); © **Digital Stock Corp.** (pp. 23 top right, 105, 140 top right); © **Dennis Dunleavy/Maryknoll Missioners** (p. 144A); © **Rachel Epstein/PhotoEdit** (p. 81 left); © **EyeWire** (pp. 40 top, 42 top); © **Myrleen Ferguson/PhotoEdit** (pp. 5, 48A); © **Chet Ha/Photographic Resources** (p. 94); © **Image Bank** (p. 100); © **Don Klumpp/Image Bank** (p. 140 bottom left and bottom right); © **Michael Newman/PhotoEdit** (pp. 81 top right, 104A); © **PhotoDisc, Inc.** (pp. 1, 10 right, 18 top right, left, and bottom right, 23 bottom right, 25 right and bottom left, 37 right, 42 middle and bottom, 68, 78 left and bottom right, 81 bottom, 88 bottom right, 104B, 123, 138–139, 140 top left); © **Eugene D. Plaisted, O.S.C./Crosiers** (pp. i, iii, 26 top, 28, 49, 61, 75, 107, 130, 133 left, 145); © **A. Ramey/PhotoEdit** (p. 74A); © **Laurent Rebours/AP/Wide World Photos** (p. 127); © **James L. Shaffer** (pp. 22 top right, 26 bottom, 41 bottom, 74C); © **Skjold Photographs** (pp. 10 left, 34, 73, 135 top); © **Erika Stone** (p. 41 top); © **W. P. Wittman Limited** (pp. 22, 23 top right and bottom left, 37 left, 40 bottom, 46, 70 top and bottom, 71–72, 78 top, 88 top right and left, 97, 101, 109, 125, 135 bottom).

Artwork (*body*)

Tim Basaldua (p. 120); **Nan Brooks** (pp. 6, 8, 12, 13, 14, 21, 64 bottom, 66 bottom, 67, 84, 86, 91, 134); **Len Ebert/PC & F Inc.** (pp. 11, 19, 29, 50, 51, 60, 66 middle, 74 top right, 82, 103, 116, 117, 128 top, 144D); **Emily Friel** (pp. 53, 77, 102 left, 128 bottom, 143); **George Hamblin/Steven Edsey & Sons** (p. 48B); **Ginna Hirtenstein** (pp. 30–31, 47, 98, 102 right, 113); **Jack Jasper** (pp. 17, 87, 92); **Melissa Kupfer** (pp. 64 top, 112, 118, 124, 132); **Polly Lewis** (pp. 54, 55 top, 56–57, 62, 63, 65, 69, 74 top left and middle and bottom, 89, 122, 131); **Maryland Cartographers** (pp. 55 bottom, 72); **Kelly Neill** (pp. 24, 27, 35); **Monica Paxson** (p. 118); **Proof Positive/Farrowlyne Assoc., Inc.** (color type pp. 4, 17, 29, 35, 59, 66, 92, 106, 108, 110, 113, 114, 141, 144); **Sally Schaedler** (pp. 3, 44–45, 76, 79, 83, 93, 95, 106, 108, 110–111, 114, 115, 119, 121, 126, 144); **Tom Sperling** (pp. 20, 32, 33, 38, 52, 58, 90, 96, 133); **Robert Voigts** (pp. 7, 16).

Artwork (*perforated section*)

Cheryl Arnemann (puzzle); **Tim Basaldua** (pp. 1, 2–3, 4 Advent Booklet; pp. 2, 3 Scripture Prayer Booklet); **Nan Brooks** (Way of the Cross Booklet, V.I.P. badge and bow punchouts); **Diana Bush** (p. 10 Scripture Prayer Booklet); **Len Ebert** (prayer cards, nativity, and tabernacle punchouts); **Emily Friel** (goldfish punchout); **Ginna Hirtenstein** (Sharing Advent as a Family); **Jack Jasper** (fish and Mary punchout buttons); **Diane Johnson** (p. 11 Scripture Prayer Booklet); **Robert Korta** (pp. 6, 7 Scripture Prayer Booklet, Jesus punchout); **Dick Mlodock** (pp. 1, 5, 8, 12 Scripture Prayer Booklet); **Monica Paxson** ("God is my Father" button, goldfish, and cross punchouts); **Robert Voigts** (A Time to Grow and Change); **Bill Wise** (color for V.I.P. badge and bow punchouts).

Cover design by Donald Kye.
Cover art © Eugene D. Plaisted, O.S.C./Crosiers.

LOYOLAPRESS.

07 WEB 7

3441 N. ASHLAND AVENUE
CHICAGO, ILLINOIS 60657
(800) 621-1008

CONTENTS

1

Goals of the Program

This program of the revised Christ Our Life series introduces your child to the goodness of God as a loving Father who has given us the gift of his own life through Baptism. Your child comes to know and love Jesus as his or her best friend. The program leads the children to a joyful awareness that the Spirit of Jesus is present in the Church and within us, calling us to speak to God our Father and to praise him by living as his children. Each lesson leads your child to a prayerful relationship with God. A Scripture prayer booklet is provided to foster your child's prayer life.

Format Designed for a Family Program

Each unit in the book begins with a summary of the message that will be presented in class. Each chapter highlights one aspect of the Christian message proclaimed in the unit. Usually a chapter is presented in class each week.

Because your faith makes a profound impact on your child, the Christ Our Life series provides a Family Corner feature, which summarizes the message of each chapter. After a chapter has been presented in class, your child will mark the box in the Family Corner. Most of the family activities suggested in the Family Corner can be done informally at mealtimes. Additional time could be taken to share the perform-a-text pages. The activities of the Family Corner are set up under four topics:

Read suggests a Scripture reference related to the topic of the chapter. The reading may be done by a parent, guardian, or older child in the family.

Discuss provides discussion topics to help you and your child apply the Scripture reading to daily life.

Pray sums up the message for the week in a short prayer that everyone can pray daily. This prayer might be printed and posted on the refrigerator or a mirror. You may add it to mealtime prayers or other family prayers.

Do provides ideas for things to discuss at meals, games to play, family activities related to the message of the chapter, and suggestions of children's storybooks (available in public libraries) to read to your child.

In addition, each unit ends with Family Feature pages that suggest family customs and provide review activities.

Educating Your Child to Live in Christ Jesus

It is our hope that as a result of the cooperative efforts of parents, children, and catechists involved in this program your child will be motivated to:

- recognize Jesus as his or her best friend and speak to him frequently each day

- respect himself or herself and every person as loved by God

- listen attentively to God's word proclaimed in the Bible and through the people who share his love

- participate meaningfully in the Sunday Mass by attentively listening to the readings and the homily; joining in the hymns, responses, and acclamations; praying the Our Father; and making a spiritual communion

- desire to be kind, fair, and honest

- ask for forgiveness when he or she has offended another

- be willing to give and share with others

- begin to realize that we are responsible for our choices and our actions

- understand and pray reverently the Sign of the Cross, the Our Father, the Hail Mary, the Doxology, and the Prayer to the Guardian Angel.

Prayer Formulas

Sign of the Cross	6
Our Father	45
Hail Mary	57
Morning Offering	88
Doxology	139
Prayer to the Guardian Angel	punchout page

God Is Our Good Father

God planned that human beings find their meaning and fulfill their destiny through Jesus Christ, his only Son. In this first unit the children are introduced to Jesus. His words and actions demonstrate that God is a loving, caring, and forgiving Father whose love calls us through our Baptism to the eternal happiness of heaven. The goodness and greatness of God, visible in the wonders of creation and in the gift of human life and freedom, are the focus of this unit.

Jesus Is Our Friend

1

We love our friends.

We like to be with them.

God is good to give us friends.

How can we be good to them?

Jesus Christ is my friend.

He likes to be with me.

Jesus said,

"Let the children come to me."
Luke 18:16

Draw yourself near Jesus.

God is good to give us Jesus.

Jesus loves everyone.

We want to be like Jesus.

We want to love others.

Draw a picture of people you love.

I love people.

Jesus' friends make the **Sign of the Cross.**

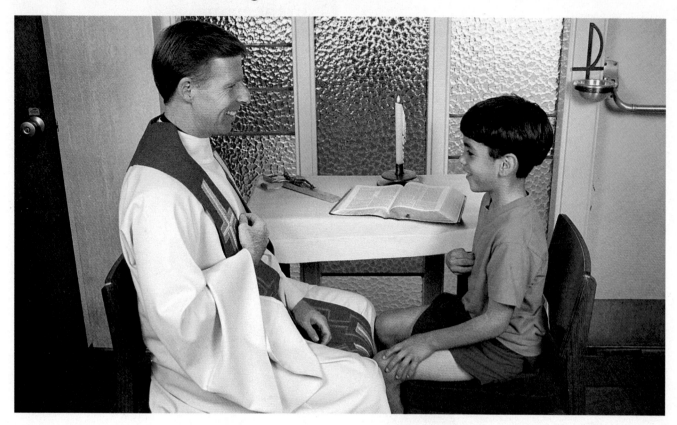

Jesus died on the cross for us.

Jesus loves us.

We make the Sign of the Cross.

We show we are Jesus' friends.

We remember Jesus loves us.

In the name
of the Father,
and of the Son,
and of the Holy Spirit.
Amen.

1

2

3

4

Color the hearts in order.

Where each heart is, say the part of the Sign of the Cross that you pray.

Why did Jesus die on the cross?
Jesus died on the cross to show how much he loves us.

Words to Know
Sign of the Cross

We Respond

I love you, Jesus.

FAMILY CORNER

Jesus invites each of us to be his friend just as he welcomed the little children of Galilee to come to him. Jesus died on the cross to show how much he loves us. We make the Sign of the Cross to show we are friends of Jesus and will try to be like him.

Read
Mark 10:13–16

Discuss
• what good things God has given our family
• how we can thank Jesus and show our love

Pray
Make the Sign of the Cross as a reminder that everything you do is in the name of the Lord.

Do
• Decide on specific times during the day to talk with Jesus.
• Display a picture of Jesus in your child's room.
• Make a cross for each room in your home. Use yarn or cord to bind two twigs in the shape of a cross. Place each cross in clay.
• Talk about how your child can take care of his or her book.
• Alert your child when the Sign of the Cross is made during Mass.
• Read a story that brings out the meaning of friendship: *My Friend Charlie* by James Flora or *Play with Me* by Marie Hall Ets.

❏ Signature

God Is Good

Our world is full of good and beautiful things.

Find some in the picture.

In the beginning God created the heavens
and the earth.

adapted from Genesis 1:1

God saw all he had made.
It was very good.

adapted from Genesis 1:31

Draw something God made new today.

The world belongs to everyone.

The beautiful things in it tell us
God is good.

God asks us to work together to
keep the world beautiful.

What can we do?

Draw a 😊 under the children who are keeping God's world good and beautiful.

A Seed

One day a little boy planted
a hard, brown seed in an
old pot.

He put the pot on the windowsill.
Every day the boy watered the seed.
Every day the sun warmed the seed.

After a while the baby plant inside the seed slowly pushed out a root.

Then the baby plant burst through the brown soil.

The little boy saw tiny green leaves.

Every day he watered the baby plant.

Every day the sun warmed the baby plant.

It grew and grew.

Then one day the boy saw a bud on the plant.

The bud slowly opened into a beautiful flower.

The boy smiled a very big smile!

He was happy he had cared for the growing seed.

Draw pretty flowers growing in the flower box.

We Remember

Who made all things?

God made all things.

We Respond

How good God is!

God made me.

God made me like himself.

I can think, choose, and love.

God made us.

He is our heavenly Father.

We are all God's children.

Draw a picture of yourself.

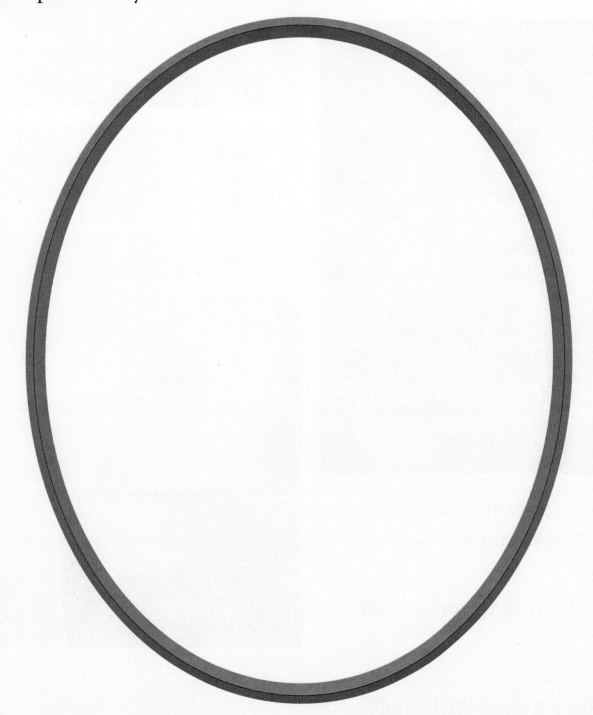

I am God's child.

A good parent loves.

A good parent cares.

A good parent forgives.

God our Father always loves
and cares for us.

He always forgives us when we
are sorry.

God is a good and loving
Father.

Trace the sentence in the clouds.

We Remember

Who is our Father in heaven?

God is our Father in heaven.

We Respond

I trust in God's love forever and ever.

adapted from Psalm 52:10

FAMILY CORNER

God continually invites us to grow and deepen our relationship with him and others. God has given us different gifts and wants us to use them to give him honor. Each of us is a unique human expression of God's kind, loving, and forgiving care.

 Read
Matthew 6:25–34

Discuss
• how prayer has helped you at times when you were afraid
• why God doesn't always give what we have asked for

 Pray
Father, give us what we need.

Do
• Tell your child what you think are God's special gifts to him or her.
• Praise your child for kind, patient, or forgiving acts.
• Read a story that shows how even little people have special gifts to share: *Pepito's Story* by Eugene Fern or *Dandelion* by Don Freeman.

❑ Signature

4

Moses was God's friend.

He knew God was holy.

Moses bowed down when he came before God.

I am God's child.

I can kneel when I talk to God
in prayer.

My actions can say to God,

"You are great and holy."

The **church** is a holy place.

Jesus is here in a special way.

We go to church to worship God.

Here are some holy things.

We see them in church.

They help us think of Jesus' love.

They help us pray to God.

Put a ✓ by what you have seen
in your church.

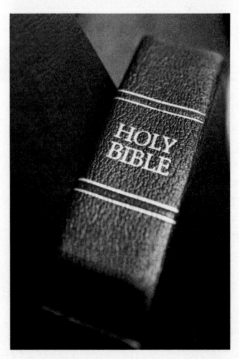

Color the church window.

Outline the cross in black.

Who is God?

God is the all-holy One.

Word to Know

church

We Respond

Holy, holy, holy Lord,
God of power and might.

FAMILY CORNER

The words and gestures we use in our worship show that we want to praise God, who is the all-holy One. The church is a sacred place where Jesus remains present in the Blessed Sacrament after Mass.

 Read
Psalm 138:1–5

Discuss
• how we can show respect toward God and other people in church

 Pray
Holy, holy, holy Lord!

Do
• Help your child pray the Holy, Holy, Holy at Sunday Mass.
• Visit church as a family and let your child explain its features. Then pray together.
• Take an inventory of the holy objects in your home, such as the Bible, crucifix, holy water, rosary, and prayer books.
• See how many ways you can name that show reverence toward God.

❏ Signature

Water is a gift from God. It is good.

Water gives life. It gives joy.

God is good to give us water.

We must take care of it.

You were baptized with **water.**

Baptism joined you to Jesus.

It gave you God's life.

God is good to share his life
with us.

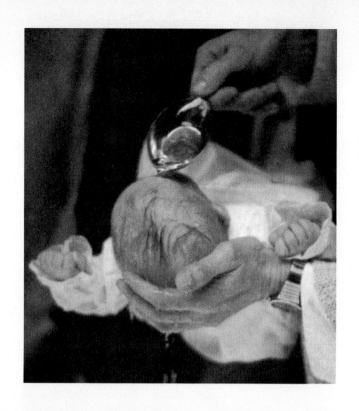

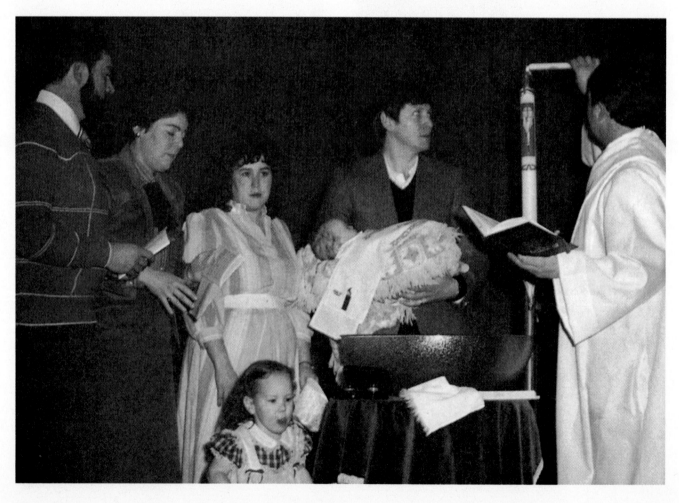

At Baptism you received your name.

Write it in pretty colors.

_____

_ _

_____

Holy oil was put on your head.

Your parents, **godparents,** and everyone else prayed for you.

You received a **white robe** and a **candle.**

They stand for God's life in us.

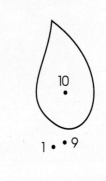

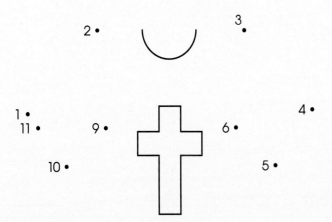

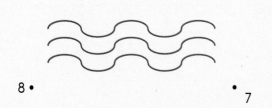

Connect the dots to draw the robe and candle.

Color the cross and the flame.

This girl has become a **Christian.**

She has God's life.

Now she belongs to God's big family.

She belongs to the **Church.**

Write the facts about your Baptism.

I received God's life. I am a Christian.

_____   _____

Day _____   Year _____

Church _____

Name _____

Draw a smile on each child of God.

Christians spread Jesus' love.

St. Julie lived long ago in France.

She liked to make people happy.

Julie became a sister.

She taught children that God is good.

What did Baptism give you?
Baptism gave me God's life.

Words to Know

Baptism   Christian

Church

We Respond

Let your love be with me, LORD.

adapted from Psalm 33:22

FAMILY CORNER

God, our good Father, shows the greatness of his love by giving us his Spirit and his own life at our Baptism. Called to live by the Spirit, we reach out to others with the love Jesus shows for us.

 Read
1 John 4:7–12

Discuss
• what we do to show we have God's life
• what we can do to get to know God better

 Pray
We want to live as your children, Lord.

Do
• Talk about your child's Baptism. Show pictures and remembrances from it.
• Mark each person's baptismal date on your family calendar. Decide how you will make those days special.
• Light a candle and let each one ask for God's light to shine more brightly.

❏ Signature

God makes wonderful things

happen in silence.

Things move.

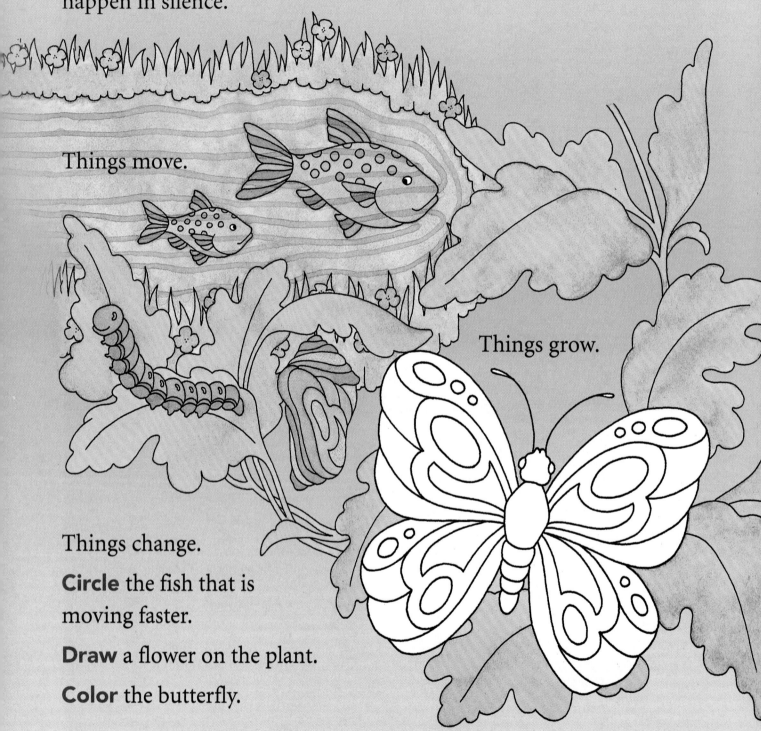

Things grow.

Things change.

Circle the fish that is
moving faster.

Draw a flower on the plant.

Color the butterfly.

We grow in silence.

We change.

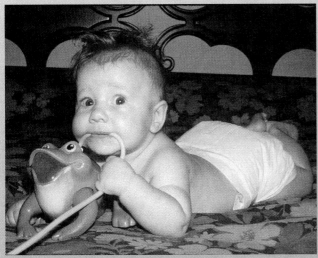

Once we were little.

Now we go to school.

We grow.

We will grow up.

God speaks to us in many ways.

God speaks in silence.

Elijah was God's friend.

He liked to talk with God.

Elijah could not hear God in the wind,

in the earthquake,   or in the fire.

Elijah heard God in the gentle breeze.

God can speak to us in silence.

God can speak to us in the quiet of our hearts.

Mother is reading the **Bible.** The children are listening carefully to God's words.

When do you listen to God's words in the Bible?

Connect the dots to finish the Bible.

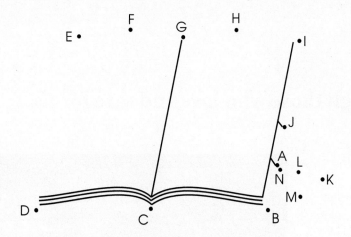

Draw a picture of a Bible story.

Here is a Bible story.

God speaks through those who love and care for us.

God gives us people who care for us.

He loves us through them.

God wants us to listen when they tell us how to be good children of God.

He wants us to try to do what they say.

God's helpers bring us his love and care.

What people bring God's love and care to you?

When do you listen to them?

Word to Know
Bible

We Remember

Who speaks to us in the Bible?
God speaks to us in the Bible.

We Respond

Your words, O God, are the joy of my heart.

adapted from Psalm 119:111

FAMILY CORNER

God enlightens and guides those who choose to follow his path of peace and love. We hear God's gentle voice in his created wonders and providential care. We listen attentively to God in the Bible, in the teachings of his Church, and in the silence of our hearts.

 Read
Matthew 7:24–27

Discuss
• why prayer is the best way to start the day
• how you can create some quiet time for talking with God

 Pray
Your words, O God, are the joy of my heart!

Do
• At mealtime prayer, thank God for the people who have shown his love toward you today.

❏ Signature

37

Samuel belonged to God's people.

God spoke to him.

Samuel listened.

Samuel spoke to God.

God listened.

Samuel was praying.

God is my Father.

God talks to me. I listen.

I talk to God. He listens.

I am **praying.**

Speak, LORD. Your child is listening.

adapted from 1 Samuel 3:10

We talk to people we love.

They listen to us.

We talk to God, our Father.

He listens to us.

We praise God.

> How good God is!
> adapted from Psalm 34:9

That's good work!

Please help me.

We ask God for help.

> O help me, LORD.
> Come quickly and help me.
> adapted from Psalm 40:14

Thank you.

We say thank you to God.

> I thank you, LORD, with all
> my heart.
>> adapted from Psalm 9:2

We tell God that we are sorry.

> LORD, I am sorry for having
> done wrong.
>> adapted from Psalm 38:19

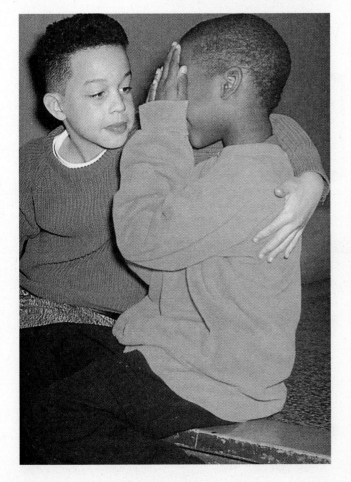

I am sorry.

We talk to our heavenly
Father every day.

We pray in the morning.

> Lord, help me do what
> is right today.

We pray at meals.

> Bless us, O Lord, and
> these your gifts.

We pray at night.

> Lord, keep me safe
> while I sleep.

Draw a picture of something you could talk to God about.

What is prayer?

Prayer is talking and listening to God.

We Respond

I call you, God, and you answer me.

adapted from Psalm 17:6

FAMILY CORNER

In prayer we consciously open ourselves to God's presence in our lives. We come to see his loving hand in all that happens to us. We take time to listen to God and to talk with him, sharing our deepest thoughts and desires.

Read
Luke 17:11–19

Discuss
• how we feel when someone thanks us
• what we want to thank God for

Pray
Thank you, Lord, for all your gifts!

Do
• Plan specific times when you will pray with your child.
• Create some device to help everyone remember to pray morning, evening, and mealtime prayers.

❏ Signature

43

The Our Father is a special prayer of God's Christian family.

Jesus gave it to us.

Jesus' friends saw him pray.

They said, "Teach us to pray."

Jesus taught them this prayer.

Our Father, who art in heaven,
    hallowed be thy name;
thy kingdom come;
thy will be done on earth
    as it is in heaven.

Give us this day our daily
    bread;
and forgive us our trespasses
    as we forgive those
    who trespass against us;
and lead us not into
    temptation,
but deliver us from evil.

                    Amen.

God's family prays the Our Father at Mass.

We can pray the Our Father when we talk
to God.

Circle seven words from the Our Father in the picture.
Number the circles in order.

We Remember

Who taught us the Our Father?
Jesus taught us the Our Father.

We Respond

Jesus, teach me to pray.

FAMILY CORNER

Jesus taught us to call God our Father and to depend with confidence on his faithful, forgiving care. Praying as Jesus taught us, we come to recognize our oneness with every person in our human family.

Read
Matthew 6:7–15

Discuss
• why it is important for us to pray every day
• why it is good for us to forgive others even though it might be hard

Pray
Our Father, who art in heaven, hallowed be thy name.

Do
• Make the Our Father part of your mealtime prayers to help your child know it by heart.
• Tell which phrase of the Our Father you like best and why. Let each member of the family take a turn.
• Talk about the temptations that make it difficult to live as children of God.

❏ Signature

Trace the path to Jesus.

What can you tell about the pictures you pass?

START

FAMILY FEATURE

Celebrating a Baptismal Anniversary

The Mahler family, who are from Germany, celebrate the anniversary of Werner's baptism, when he became a child of God and received divine life. Each year on that day they display Werner's baptismal certificate, baptismal garment, candle, and cards on the mantel or on the living room table. Werner's parents talk about the day and how they chose his name while they go through pictures of the ceremony in their family photo album.

For dinner that day the Mahlers prepare Werner's favorite meal: roast beef, mashed potatoes with gravy, green beans, strawberry ice cream, and a special cake. Werner's godparents come for dinner. Sometimes Father Hanzo, who baptized Werner, is able to come too. Everyone says grace together, holding hands around the table as a sign of unity in God's family.

The Mahlers try to celebrate Mass together on that day at church or with a home Mass. Before or after the meal they have a special prayer service. The baptismal candle is lit. Werner's parents and godparents renew their commitment to help him be a strong Christian and follow the way of Jesus, and Werner renews his baptismal promises by rejecting sin and evil and promising to live like Jesus. The godparents say to Werner, "Safeguard the grace of your baptism by living a blameless life. Keep the commandments so that when the Lord comes again, you may be worthy to join all the saints in heaven." Then all pray the Apostles' Creed together.

You may wish to begin the tradition of baptismal anniversary celebrations in your family. It is an excellent way to keep your child mindful of the gift of faith. It also binds family members more closely together.

We Pray

A Christian child prays. In each circle paste or draw something for which you especially wish to praise and thank God. Each family member might do one or two.

I praise and thank you, God, for . . .

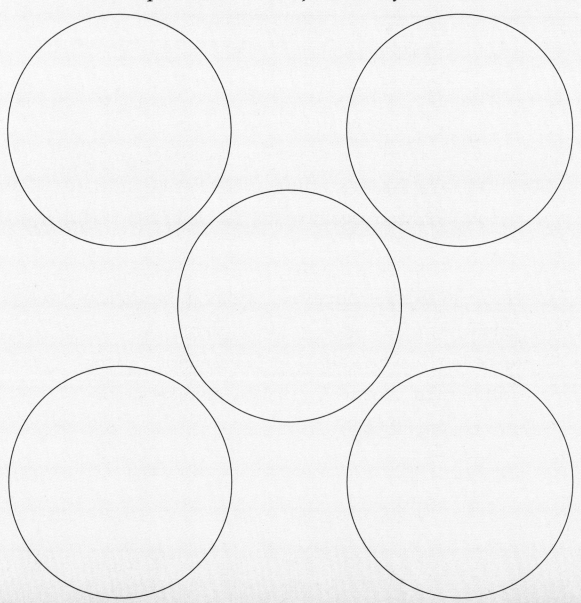

God Sent His Son as Our Savior

In this unit the children learn about God's goodness and mercy shown in his promise of a Savior. They are taught about God's gifts to Adam and Eve and their destiny to live with him forever. They learn how sin changed God's plan but brought the promise of a redeemer, the Son of God, who would win back for our human family a share in God's life and the possibility of eternal happiness in heaven.

The Bible tells a story about the first people on earth.

God made Adam and Eve.

Adam and Eve were happy.

They were God's friends.

God was good to Adam and Eve.

He shared his life with them.

They could be happy with God in **heaven.**

They would live forever.

Draw flowers, fruit, birds, and animals to make the garden more beautiful.

But Adam and Eve did not obey God.

Then they lost **grace,** God's life.

They were no longer God's friends.

They were sad.

God still loved Adam and Eve.

God said, "I will send a **Savior.**

He will help you be my friends again."

Then Adam and Eve were happy.

Copy the missing words on the lines.

God chose a people.

He chose the

_____

- - - - - - - - - - - - - - -

_____ .

Jewish people

He told them to get ready for the

_____

- - - - - - - - - - - - - - -

_____ .

Savior

God's people waited and prayed.

Whom would God send?

Write the first letter of each picture in the box.

What promise did God make to Adam and Eve?

God promised to send a Savior.

Words to Know

heaven   grace   Savior

We Respond

Save us, LORD God, please save us.

adapted from Psalm 40:14

FAMILY CORNER

God showed divine mercy when the parents of our human family used their freedom to oppose his will. Although they had offended God's love, he promised a redeemer who would save the world from the effects of sin.

 Read
Genesis 3:1–19

Discuss
- which things we do that keep us near God and happy
- which things we or others do that make us unhappy and why
- at what particular times each of us can say yes to God
- when your doing good brought happiness to another person

 Pray
Come, Lord Jesus!

Do
- Make an Advent wreath or put up one your child made in class.
- See "Sharing Advent as a Family" at the back of this book and select other Advent projects.
- Help your child recall times when he or she may have tried to hide having done something wrong. Talk about better ways to handle the situations.
- Read or tell a story that shows how children can take the lead in restoring good family relationships or friendships: *The Accident* by Carol Carrick, *I'm Not Oscar's Friend Anymore* by Marjorie Sharmat, or *The Hating Book* by Charlotte Zolotow.

❑ Signature

Mary belonged to God's people.

The angel Gabriel came to her.

He said, "Hail Mary, full of grace!

God has chosen you to be the mother of the Savior.

You will name him Jesus."

Mary said, "Yes, I will do what God wants."

Mary got ready for Jesus.

Jesus is God's Son.

Jesus is God.

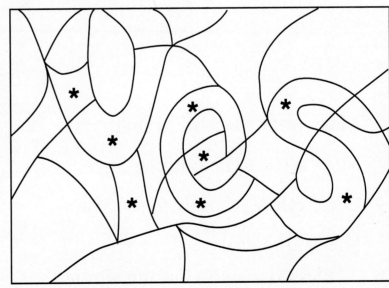

Color the pieces marked *.

See what Mary said to God.

Mary went to visit Elizabeth.

Mary went to help her relative.

Elizabeth was happy to see Mary.

She said to Mary,
   "Blessed are you among women."

Mary is the Mother of God.

We pray to her.

Here is a prayer that you can learn.

Hail Mary, full of grace!
The Lord is with you.
Blessed are you among women,
    and blessed is the fruit
    of your womb, Jesus.
Holy Mary, Mother of God,
    pray for us sinners,
    now and at the hour of our death.
                                Amen.

Find the angel Gabriel's words to Mary in the prayer.

Now find Elizabeth's words to Mary.

Joseph belonged to God's people.

He was a good man.

He did what was right.

God chose him to care for Jesus and Mary.

He was the foster father of Jesus.

Joseph loved Jesus and Mary.

He worked hard for his family.

Joseph was a carpenter.

Draw something Joseph may have made out of wood.

God has chosen people to love and care for us.

What people love you?

Draw a picture of the people who love you.

How do you love and thank them for their care?

People love me.

Draw a line to the answer that matches.

Told Mary she would
be Jesus' mother •

Foster father of Jesus •

What Mary said to God •

Mother of God •

Mary's Son, the Savior •

• Yes

We Remember

Who is the Mother of God?
Mary is the Mother of God.

We Respond

Hail Mary, full of grace!
The Lord is with you.

FAMILY CORNER

God kept his promise to send a Savior. Mary was chosen to be the Mother of the Son of God. Joseph also was chosen to care for Jesus. Both Mary and Joseph show us how we can prepare for Christ's coming into our hearts.

Read
Luke 1:26–45

Discuss
• how Mary was helpful to Elizabeth
• various opportunities you had to say yes to God today
• how each one in your family can be helpful to the others

Pray
Jesus, Mary, Joseph!

Do
• Visit a person who is sick or lonely. Make a gift to take with you or decide what family talents can be shared during the visit.
• Help your child learn the Hail Mary. Pray it aloud together each day. Decide on a family time when you can pray a decade of the rosary.
• Explain why you hope your child will pray for you.
• Read *My Mother Is the Most Beautiful Woman in the World*, a Russian folktale retold by Becky Reyher in book form.

❏ Signature

Christmas is a time for gifts.

It is a time to show love.

It is a time for the story of the first Christmas.

God gave the first Christmas present.

He gave his Son Jesus to be our Savior.

God showed how much he loved us.

Mary and Joseph went to Bethlehem.

This was God's plan.

Jesus was born in a stable.

Mary wrapped him in warm clothes.

Angels sang,
"Glory to God in the highest."

Shepherds came to see Jesus.

This is Christmas—
Jesus, God's Son, comes into
our world.

Wise men in the East saw a special star.

They followed it to where Jesus was.

The wise men gave him gifts.

They told others the Good News.

Jesus is our Savior.

He came to save all people.

Draw a star in the sky.

Make it shine.

Christmas is Jesus' birthday.

Draw a gift you will give to him.

Write the right words on the lines.

1. The _____ told the shepherds about Jesus.

   manger

2. Only in a _____ was there room for Mary and Joseph.

   wise men

3. Jesus lay in a _____ .

   stable

4. A _____ was over the place where Jesus lay.

   angel

5. The star led the _____ .

   star

Use the code to find the secret message.

A	D	E	G	I	J	M	N	O	S	U
1	2	3	4	5	6	7	8	9	10	11

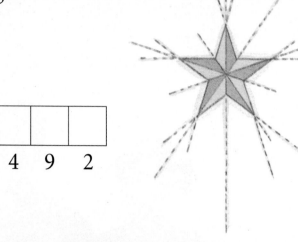

6	3	10	11	10

5	10

4	9	2

1	8	2

7	1	8
.

We Remember

When was Jesus our Savior born?
Jesus our Savior was born on Christmas Day.

Word to Know
Christmas

We Respond

Glory to God in the highest.

FAMILY CORNER

God sent his Son to save us. God the Son emptied himself and became human like us in all things except sin. When Jesus was born in Bethlehem, the Savior's arrival was announced to shepherds by angels, who told them to share the Good News with others.

 Read
Luke 2:1–20; Matthew 2:1–12

Discuss
• why it is sometimes difficult to obey
• what made the shepherds happy
• why the gift of ourselves is better than any gift money can buy
• what your family can do to bring the Good News about Jesus to others

 Pray
Glory to you, O God!

Do
• Plan a family or community Christmas caroling fest. Enjoy snacks afterward.
• Ask your child to tell the story presented on pages 62 and 63 of this book.
• Use the celebration on pages 66 and 67, going in procession to your family crib scene, carrying lighted candles to welcome the Savior, the light of the world.
• See how many words in the Christmas story your child can think of and tell about.

❏ Signature

We celebrate the birth of Jesus.

Come, let us adore.

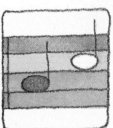 **Song** "O Come, All Ye Faithful"

 **Reading** Mary and Joseph went to Bethlehem.

They looked for a room.

There was no room anywhere.

They went to a stable.

There Jesus was born.

Mary laid him in a manger.

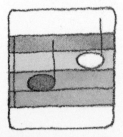 **Song** "Happy Birthday, Dear Jesus"

Glory to you, O God!

Reading An angel came to the shepherds.

He said,
   "Jesus is born.
   He is in Bethlehem.
   He is lying in a manger."

Angels sang,
   "Glory to God."

Then they left.

The shepherds went quickly
to see Jesus.

How happy they were!

We thank you, God our Father!

Our Gifts "I love you, Jesus."

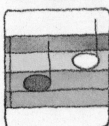

Song "Silent Night, Holy Night"

We belong to a family.

We do things together.

Each person in our family is special.

We need one another.

We love one another.

Jesus belonged to the **Holy Family.**

Each person was special.

They all loved one another.

Jesus' family did things together.

They worked and played together.

They prayed together.

The Holy Family was a happy family.

Copy the names of the people in the Holy Family.

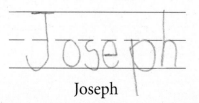

Jesus   Mary   Joseph

A **parish** is a special kind of family.

Priests, sisters, and many other people belong to a parish family.

Because we are baptized, we belong to the Church family.

Draw a line to the right picture.

People •

Priest •

Sister •

The name of my parish is

St. John

People in our parish family care about one another.

We go to **Mass** to worship together.

We listen to God's words in the Bible.

We remember that Jesus died and rose for us.

We thank God for being so good to us.

Jesus is with us.

He offers himself to the Father for us.

The parish family likes to pray
and sing together.

Color the words.

AMEN,
AMEN,
AMEN!

Write the letters that come just before the ones in the boxes.

You will see a prayer.

H	P	E
G	O	D

C	M	F	T	T
B	L	e	s	s

N	Z
M	y

G	B	N	J	M	Z
F	A	M	I	L	y

We Remember

Why does God give us families?
God gives us families so that we can love and help one another.

Words to Know
Holy Family   parish   Mass

We Respond

How good it is to live together in love.

adapted from Psalm 133:1

FAMILY CORNER

Jesus, Mary, and Joseph were a happy family because they were united in God's love. Many little deeds of love created the joyful sharing and caring spirit of the Holy Family.

 Read
Matthew 18:23–25

Discuss
• how each person in your family is needed
• how each person in your family is special and brings joy to others
• how everyone needs forgiveness and how you as a family can make up each evening

 Pray
May God bless us and keep us!

Do
• Put a note under family members' plates thanking them for something they did recently that brought joy to the family.
• Recall your family rules and discuss how they help make family life happier. Let each person decide on one thing he or she can do better.
• Talk about what your family can do to make each Mass a parish family celebration of worship.
• Read a story that shows ways children brought happiness to the family: *Send Wendell* by Genevieve Gray, *Benjie* by Joan Lexau, or *Peggy's New Brother* by Eleanor Schick.

❑ Signature

Number the pictures in order from 1 to 6.

Tell the stories, taking turns.

FAMILY FEATURE

A Christmas Posada

Every Christmas the Riveras in Mexico join the nine-day posada in their neighborhood. Posada means "inn" or "shelter." Beginning at dusk, people go from door to door, reenacting Mary and Joseph's search for a place to stay in Bethlehem. This year seven-year-old Elena will dress as the angel who knocks at each door asking whether there is any room. Her cousins, José and Juan, will carry a tray holding statues of Mary and Joseph encircled by evergreens.

As the group processes, the people sing carols about the first Christmas. At house after house, people come to the door to say that there is no room. Finally at one house the children are told, "Enter, holy pilgrims. This night is one of joy, for we shelter the Mother of God." Everyone enters and kneels in prayer, asking that the Christ Child may enter their homes and hearts. Then refreshments are served, and the children take turns swinging with a stick at a piñata filled with candy and prizes. When the piñata is broken open, its treasures are shared by all.

You may wish to adopt this custom. Invite
friends to participate with you in celebrating a
neighborhood posada. Or you may celebrate
within your own home by processing around
your house knocking on different doors. A
family member could play the innkeeper.

A Christ Tree

Work together to decorate the Christmas tree as a Christ tree. Draw ornaments related to Jesus, the Savior. Refer to the stories of the first Christmas in Luke 2:1–20 and Matthew 2:1–12.

Jesus Shows Us He Is Good

Unit 3 presents the Father's love through the words and deeds of Jesus in his public life. The children learn that Jesus teaches us to love God with all our hearts and to love others as he loves us. They see Jesus' concern for us as he reaches out to heal, to encourage, and to dispel fear. They hear Jesus call them to be apostles and to continue his ministry of healing and reconciliation.

Jesus grew up.

He told people about his Father.

He called twelve **apostles** to help spread the Good News of God's love.

Jesus wanted everyone to know how good and loving his Father is.

Finish the story.
Use the words in the fish.

_____

_ _ _ _ _ _ _ _ _ _ _ _

Jesus called _____ and

_____

_ _ _ _ _ _ _ _ _ _

_____ .

_____

_ _ _ _ _ _ _ _ _ _

He called _____ and

_____

_ _ _ _ _ _ _ _ _ _ _

_____ .

_____

_ _ _ _ _ _ _ _ _

Today Jesus calls _____
to be apostles.

James

John

us

Andrew

Peter

Jesus calls all Christians to help build a better world.

He wants the whole world to be full of God's goodness.

Many people work together to bring God's love and care into our world.

Mothers and fathers help children grow in God's love.

Priests, deacons, brothers, and sisters show God's love in a special way.

Rulers of countries work for peace.

Farmers grow food for God's big family.

Workers make things people need.

Artists make beautiful things.

What other helpers work to make our world better?

What can you do?

Jesus took care of his apostles.

He stopped a bad storm when they were afraid.

Jesus takes care of us today.

He is with us when we are afraid.

He may send someone to help us.

He may want us to ask someone for help.

Jesus helps us through other people.

To whom can you go for help?

St. Frances Cabrini lived in Italy long ago.

She wanted to tell people in faraway lands about God.

She crossed the ocean and came to the United States.

She formed a group of sisters.

They worked in schools and hospitals.

We Remember

What does Jesus call Christians to do?

Jesus calls Christians to work together to bring all people to him and to make the world a better place.

We Respond

May the whole earth be filled with God's love.

adapted from Psalm 72:19

FAMILY CORNER

Jesus chose twelve simple men to be his first apostles. We too are called to walk with Jesus and to share his peace and joy with others.

 Read
Luke 5:1–11

Discuss
- times when you heard the Lord call you to do something
- times when you realized that the Lord was helping you
- various ways Jesus helped people, showing them the power of God
- what you can do to bring others to know God's love

 Pray
Thy kingdom come!

Do
- Pray that priests and religious will be generous in their following of Christ.
- Pray every day for a person who has influenced your life.
- Adopt a missionary. Write regularly and offer the support of prayer and sacrifice.
- Invite a priest or religious to your home to share a meal and to explain what priestly or religious life is like.
- Tell how someone has been an apostle to you.
- Discuss the talents family members can use as they strive to be apostles.
- Tell some ways various people you know have followed Jesus.

❏ Signature

God made the world good, but some things in our world are not good.

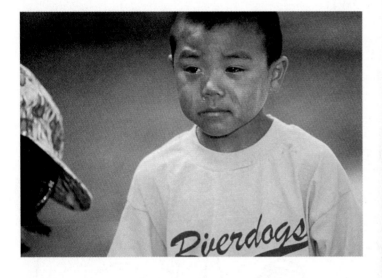

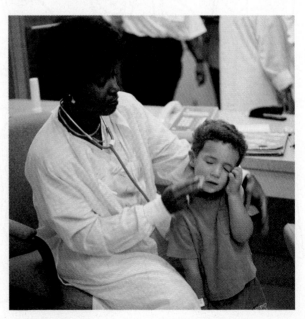

People suffer and cry.

People are hungry and lonely.

People hurt others.

We all feel sadness and pain.

God our Father loves us.

He sent Jesus to be a friend of poor and suffering people.

The Bible tells how Jesus showed God's love for people.

Here is one story.

One man could not move at all.

Friends brought him on a mat to Jesus.

Jesus was teaching a crowd in a house.

The men made a hole in the roof and let their friend down.

Jesus forgave the man for doing wrong.

Then Jesus told the man to get up and walk.

The man stood up.

Color the picture.

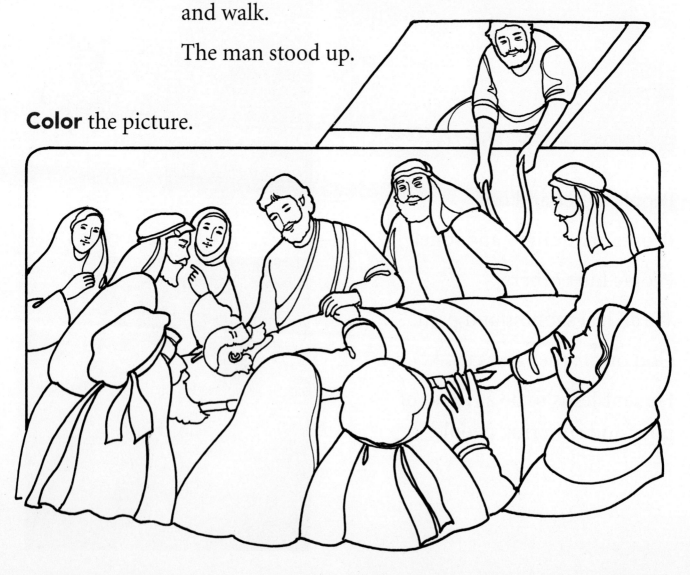

Match the sentences with the pictures.
Write the correct number in each box.

1. Jesus healed sick people.

2. Jesus forgave people who had done wrong.

3. Jesus told people that God loved them.

4. Jesus gave food to hungry people.

Jesus brings God's love to others today.

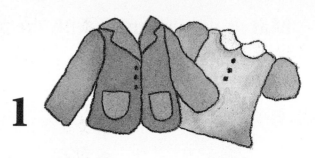

Write on each line the number of the picture that completes the sentence.

Jesus heals when _____ care for people.

Jesus feeds the hungry when we share _____ .

Jesus tells of God's love when a _____ tells about God.

Jesus helps the poor when people share _____ .

Write e in each ◯, **o** in each ▢, and **i** in each △.

J◯sus l▢ved h△s fr△◯nds.

H◯ car◯d ab▢ut all p◯▢pl◯.

J◯sus h◯als p◯▢pl◯ t▢day.

J◯sus △s th◯ S▢n ▢f G▢d.

We Remember

Who shows God's love for people?
Jesus shows God's love for people.

We Respond

Jesus, help me to bring God's love to our world.

FAMILY CORNER

Jesus spent his life doing good. With tender compassion he comforted and healed the sick and the suffering. The Church today continues Christ's works of love.

Read
Mark 1:40–43

Discuss

- in what way you think Jesus looked at the sick man
- particular things you can do to help a sick or unhappy person
- how God has brought good from the suffering that entered your life or the lives of those you love

Pray
Hear my cry for help
my king, my God!
Psalm 5:3

Do

- Adopt an elderly or lonely person and do things with and for him or her throughout the year.
- Transport someone to the Anointing of the Sick in your parish.
- Make new neighbors feel welcome.
- At mealtime each evening share a good thing that someone did for you that day.
- See how many Gospel stories you can name that show Jesus' care and concern for others.
- Make a collage from pictures showing people helping others.

_____

❏ Signature

One day a man asked Jesus,

"What is the greatest law of God?"

Jesus said,

"You shall love God with all your heart."

adapted from Mark 12:28–30

Jesus loved God his Father.

Jesus talked to God.

He always did what his Father wanted.

How can we show we love God our Father too?

Draw lines from the sentences to the correct pictures.

We can obey.　　We can go to Mass.　　We can pray.

Draw yourself doing something that shows God you love him.

Copy the prayer on the lines.

_____

_ _ _ _ _ _ _ _ _ _ _ _ _ _ _ _ _

_____

I love you, Lord.

Jesus offers himself to God each day at Mass.
We offer ourselves to God too.
We can pray the Morning Offering.

Copy the missing words.

O Jesus, I offer you all I

_____

think,

_____

do,

and

_____

say.

Bless me and make me like you today.

St. John the apostle loved Jesus very much.

He stayed with Jesus when he died on the cross.

Then he took care of Mary.

He taught people to love God and one another.

John's teachings are in the Bible.

What is the greatest law?
The greatest law is
"You shall love God with
all your heart."

We Respond

I love you, LORD.

Psalm 18:2

FAMILY CORNER

Love for his Father prompted Christ to converse with him in prayer and to fulfill his will. God's love for us calls for a response of love.

Read
John 14:21–23

Discuss
• how you as a family can make more room for God in your lives
• why obeying God's laws shows love for him
• why it is so difficult at times to love
• how your family shows that God comes first in your lives

Pray
My God, I love you!

Do
• Help your child make prayer an important part of every day.
• Print the prayer found on page 88 in this book. Post it on your mirror and say it every morning and evening.
• At supper share some of the thoughts, words, and actions of the day that were offered as pleasing gifts to God.
• Name words and gestures we use to worship God.

_____

❏ Signature

Jesus told a story to explain God's second great law.

A man was hurt and needed help.
Two men passed by him.
Then a kind man stopped and helped him.
Jesus tells us to be like the kind man.
He tells us to love our neighbor.

Jesus told us that everyone is our neighbor.

We try to help everyone in need.

What do these people need?

Find the word in the Word Box and print it on the line.

food   help

friend   visit

Draw yourself doing something
that shows you love others.

I love others.

A poor woman went to the Temple.

She gave two coins in the offering box.

Jesus saw her.

He praised her for giving what she had.

We Remember

What is the second great law of God?
The second great law is "You shall love your neighbor as yourself."

We Respond

Lord God, fill me with your love.

FAMILY CORNER

Jesus showed the meaning of Christian love by his own example. We learn what the command to love our neighbor implies through his parable of the Good Samaritan.

Read
Luke 10:25–37

Discuss
- how you feel when someone ignores you
- how your family can help a disabled person
- what sad, lonely, or frightened person your family can help
- what talents and material goods you can share with others

Pray
Praise the LORD, who is so good!
Psalm 136:1

Do
- Heal someone's hurt today by words and deeds of kindness.
- Decide on a sacrifice you will make to give money to feed hungry children.
- Print these words and post them: "What you do to others, you do to me."
- Make a mission bank to keep on your kitchen table.
- Renew yourselves listening to one another and being sensitive to every family member's needs.
- Read or tell a story that helps children understand the joy that kindness brings: *Talking without Words* by Marie Hall Ets or *Kindness Is a Lot of Things* by Edith Eckblad.

❑ Signature

Good shepherds love and care for their sheep.

They feed them and keep them from harm.

Sheep know their shepherd.

They come when their shepherd calls them.

They listen to him.

They follow him.

Sometimes a sheep may get lost.

A good shepherd finds it and brings it back.

Jesus says,

"I am the good shepherd."

John 10:11

Jesus calls us.

We go to him when we pray.

We listen when he tells us to be loving.

We follow him by doing what he asks.

But sometimes we do not follow Jesus.

We do things we know are wrong.

We are like lost lambs.

Then we are sorry.

Jesus always forgives us.

He brings us back to his love.

Here is a prayer from the Bible.

David, a shepherd boy, probably wrote it.

The LORD is my shepherd.
There is nothing that I need.
He leads me to green grass and
    fresh waters.
He guides me on right paths.
I will not be afraid, for you are
    with me.
Your goodness and kindness
        will be with me
    every day of my life.
And I will live in your home
        forever.

adapted from Psalm 23

Jesus is the Good Shepherd of God's family, the Church.

At Mass we say we are sorry that we have not always followed Jesus.

We say,
    "Lord, have mercy."

We mean,
    "Lord, forgive us and
    help us."

We give signs of peace and love to others.

We show we are happy that God has forgiven us.

We forgive one another.

Circle the sheep hidden in the picture.
Think about the ways Jesus looks for us.

We Remember

Who said, "I am the good shepherd"?
Jesus said,

"I am the good shepherd."
John 10:11

We Respond

The LORD is my shepherd.
There is nothing that I need.
adapted from Psalm 23:1

FAMILY CORNER

The forgiving love of our God is revealed through the words and actions of Jesus. Through him we hear God telling us how happy he is when we come back and say we are sorry for doing what is wrong.

 Read
John 10:2–5, 14–15

Discuss
• what you can do to hear Jesus, your Good Shepherd, every day
• how Jesus, the Good Shepherd, brings us back to him after we have done wrong
• why it is good to turn to God in prayer when sad things happen
• special ways God has shown his care for your family

 Pray
The LORD is my shepherd.
There is nothing that I need.
adapted from Psalm 23:1

Do
• Every day pray Psalm 23 found on page 96 in this book.
• Help your child to understand and appreciate that spiritual gifts are better than things money can buy.
• Explain how you, like the Good Shepherd, always love your child, even when he or she is mean or naughty.
• Share your favorite sayings of Jesus and learn them by heart.

❏ Signature

God tells his big family to love
him and one another.

It is not always easy to be kind.

It is not always easy to obey.

It is not always easy to do what
God wants us to do.

It is not always easy to be a friend
of Jesus.

Sometimes we hurt others.

We are sorry.

We can say we are sorry.

> Sometimes others hurt us.
>
> We forgive them.
>
> Then we are good friends of Jesus.

Sometimes we come together as God's
family, the Church, to say that we are sorry.

We tell God that we are sorry.

We tell one another that we are sorry.

We ask God to help us be like Jesus.

We say, "We are sorry, Lord,

✠ for the times we did not show love,

✠ for the times we hurt others,

✠ for the times we did not obey, and

✠ for the times we were selfish."

Turn your book upside down.

You will see how we feel when we are forgiven.

What do we do when we have not shown love?

When we have not shown love, we say, "I'm sorry."

We Respond

Jesus, forgive me.

FAMILY CORNER

In a celebration of forgiveness, new bonds of love are created between God, ourselves, and others. We reach out to others with a forgiving heart as a sign of our union with the Lord, in whom we are all one.

Read
Luke 15:1–7

Discuss
- how you feel when someone is sorry for having done wrong
- why adults need to be forgiven too
- the difference between deliberately doing something wrong and having an accident
- how many people feel when they have been forgiven for a misunderstanding and/or deliberate meanness

Pray
Lord, grant us peace!

Do
- Help your child identify the reasons why he or she does mean or selfish things.
- Help your child participate in the Penitential Rite of the Mass and the Sign of Peace.
- Name people who act like good shepherds and tell how they care for others.
- Read a story that shows that happiness results when sorrow is expressed and an offense is forgiven: *Wait for William* by Marjorie Flack, *Mr. Tall and Mr. Small* by Barbara Brenner, or *The Old Witch Goes to the Ball* by Ida DeLage.

❏ Signature

Jesus' Two Great Commandments

1 Love God

2 Love others

Put a **1** in the box if the picture shows how we love God.

Put a **2** in the box if the picture shows how we love others.

Draw the story of the lost sheep.

1

A man had a hundred sheep.

2

He lost one.

3

He found the sheep and carried it home.

4

He had a party with his friends.

FAMILY FEATURE

A Place at the Table for Christ

On Sundays and special feasts like Easter, Thanksgiving, and Christmas, the Reillys practice a Gaelic custom. They set a place at the table for Christ. He may come as a stranger, a passerby, or an unexpected family member. Last year Mr. Jaxon, the next-door neighbor whose wife was in the hospital, joined the Reillys for Thanksgiving dinner. On Easter Mrs. Reilly invited the parish organist who has no relatives in town. When the family was celebrating Tom's eighth birthday, a young man came to the door asking whether the Reillys had seen his lost dog. He stayed for the birthday meal. On days when the extra place is not filled, it reminds the Reillys of the Lord's presence among them.

You might wish to begin this tradition and fulfill the Lord's wish expressed in Isaiah:

This, rather, is the fasting that I wish. . . .

Sharing your bread with the hungry,

   sheltering the oppressed and the homeless;

Clothing the naked when you see them,

   and not turning your back on your own.

Isaiah 58:6–7

If you bestow your bread on the hungry

   and satisfy the afflicted;

Then light shall rise for you in the darkness. . . .

Then the LORD will guide you always

   and give you plenty.

Isaiah 58:10–11

A Time-to-Be-Kind Calendar

For each day of the next month write in a special act of kindness each family member could try to do. For Sundays you might plan to do a kind deed for someone together as a family. Let your child decorate the space at the top. Keep the calendar on the refrigerator.

SUNDAY	MONDAY	TUESDAY	WEDNESDAY	THURSDAY	FRIDAY	SATURDAY

Jesus Shows His Great Love

Unit 4 presents the Paschal Mystery: how Christ, by his suffering, death, and resurrection, reconciled our human family to God. It presents Jesus as he is with us today through his Spirit. The children learn of the beginnings of the Church, its mission to spread the Gospel, and Mary's place as the Mother of the Church. They become aware of how the Holy Spirit leads them to become holy, to spread the Good News, and to give glory to God.

Passion Sunday

Have you ever seen a parade?

People march and bands play.

We wave flags and cheer.

Long ago a parade honored Jesus.

People put their cloaks on the street.

Jesus rode along the street on a donkey.

People waved palm branches.

They shouted, "Hosanna" to Jesus.

They wanted to make Jesus king.

Holy Week is a special time for God's family, the Church.

The Church remembers important happenings in Jesus' life.

On Passion Sunday the Church remembers the parade that honored Jesus.

Draw a line from each sentence to the missing word.

Jesus is our ___.   •   • branches

We pray and sing to ___. •   • Sunday

We carry palm ___.   •   • king

It is Passion ___.   •   • Jesus

Holy Thursday

Gifts are a part of celebrations.

There are birthday gifts, Christmas gifts, and going-away gifts.

A gift is a way of showing love.

Write the words in the story.

The night before he died, Jesus celebrated a meal with his friends.

At this last supper, he gave all his friends a gift.

The gift was himself.

Jesus took _____ .
                    bread

He said, "This is my Body."

He took a cup of _____ .
                       wine

He said, "This is my Blood."

Jesus gave himself to his friends as bread and wine.

He gave them **Holy Communion.** He told them,

"Do this in memory of me."
Luke 22:19

At Mass the priest does what Jesus did.

He says,
 "This is my Body. This is my Blood."

_____

_ _ _ _ _ _ _ _ _

The bread and wine become _____ .

Jesus

Jesus offers himself to the Father.

Then he gives us the gift of himself.

He gives Holy Communion to God's people.

Jesus is with us in the tabernacle.

He is there as the Bread of Life.

We belong to God's people.

We will receive Jesus in Holy Communion.

Good Friday

Jesus died on the cross for us.

Copy the prayer.

I love you,

Jesus

my Savior.

Jesus showed how much he loved his Father.

He showed how much God loves us.

Jesus showed how much he loves us.

He gave his life for us.

On the cross, he gave us Mary for a mother.

Jesus died and rose to free us from sin.

Now we have new life.

We can bring Jesus' love to our world.

We can be happy in heaven forever.

Draw lines to match the days with the pictures.

Passion Sunday •

Holy Thursday •

Good Friday •

We Remember

What gift does Jesus give us at Mass?

Jesus gives us himself in the blessed bread and wine at Mass.

Why is Jesus our Savior?

Jesus is our Savior because he died and rose to save us from sin and win us new life.

We Respond

Give thanks to the LORD, for he is good.

His love lasts forever.

adapted from Psalm 118:1

FAMILY CORNER

At the Last Supper Jesus gave us the Eucharist. He loved us so much that he redeemed us by his blood. At Mass he continues to offer himself to the Father and to nourish us. He makes us one with himself and one another.

Read
Luke 23:33–49

Discuss
• how we show love for God at Mass
• how you can make a spiritual communion
• ways you might be mocked for following Jesus and how you feel about it

Pray
O Christ, by your holy cross you have redeemed the world!

Do
• Ask your child to help you bake bread. In a celebration thank God for food, especially the Bread of Life.
• Invite a priest home to celebrate the Eucharist, or carry the gifts at a parish Mass.
• Pray one station of the cross each evening. Relate it to difficulties you faced that day.
• Make the hours from twelve to three on Good Friday sacred.

❏ Signature

Easter

Birds sing.

Flowers bloom.

Bunnies hop.

New life is everywhere.

Alleluia! Alleluia! Alleluia!

New life in the spring reminds us of Jesus' new life.

He rose from the dead on Easter Sunday with new life!

He had a glorified body.

He visited his friends.

The risen Jesus is with us today.

He is with us in the **Eucharist.**

He is with us in all things that are good and beautiful.

He brings new life to those who believe in him.

Two friends of Jesus did not know that he had risen.

They were sad.

While they were walking down a road, a kind man met them.

He asked, "Why are you sad?"

"Jesus has died," they told him.

The man said, "Jesus had to die to bring new life."

The two friends asked the kind man to stay with them.

At supper he blessed the bread, broke it, and gave it to the friends.

Then they knew that the man was Jesus.

How happy they were!

Trace the bread and color it brown.

Jesus, our risen Savior, is with us.

These pictures show where we can meet him.

Connect the dots.

Jesus visited his apostles on Easter evening.

He said, "Peace be with you. If you forgive people's sins, they are forgiven."

Jesus gives peace to his friends. He wants his friends to bring peace to others.

How can you bring Jesus' peace to someone today?

Is the child in each picture giving peace?

Print Yes or No.

"That was a good dinner, Mom."

Yes

"You can't play with my game."

No

"Dad, would you like to see the paper?"

Yes

"Let me help you find the pictures."

Yes

For Jesus
Draw yourself praying
to Jesus.

For Others
Draw yourself bringing peace
to others.

Write the letter of the correct word on the line.

1. The Last Supper was on ____ .   **A.** Jesus

2. Jesus changed bread and wine into ____ .   **B.** himself

3. Jesus made his apostles ____ .   **C.** priests

4. At Mass priests act and speak for ____ .   **D.** Holy Thursday

5. At the Eucharist ____ become Jesus.   **E.** sin

6. On Easter Jesus gave us the gift of ____ .   **F.** Easter

7. Jesus died to save us from ____ .   **G.** bread and wine

8. Jesus rose from the dead on ____ .   **H.** peace

Here is a story about Thomas.

Draw lines to the missing words.

Thomas did not see Jesus on ____. •   • side

Thomas was not ____. •   • Thomas

He did not ____. •   • God

Jesus came to see ____. •   • Easter

He showed his hands and ____. •   • there

Thomas said, "My Lord and my ____." •   • believe

Pray about these pictures.

We Remember

When did Jesus rise from the dead?

Jesus rose from the dead on Easter Sunday.

We Respond

Alleluia! Jesus is risen and is with us.

Word to Know

Eucharist

FAMILY CORNER

Christ's resurrection reveals that God's love is stronger than death. Jesus is still with us. Through the Paschal Mystery (his passion, death, and resurrection) the new life of Christ is possible for us. The Paschal Mystery is the mystery of God's love inviting us to live in the hope and joy of the risen Lord.

Read
Luke 24:13–43

Discuss
- times when you didn't recognize the ways in which Jesus came into your life
- what each family member can do to bring more peace into daily family life
- the joys people gain through death, especially new life with Jesus
- how loved ones who have died want us to feel about their going to God
- how loved ones who have died still care for us

Pray
My Lord and my God!

Do
- Decorate your dining room with a baptismal candle and robe. Tell God how you want to live as his children.
- See how many signs of new life you can associate with Easter.
- Discuss the sacrifices your family made during Lent and help your child recognize the good that came from each.
- Make up riddles about Easter symbols. See who can guess your symbol.
- Decorate Easter eggs with symbols of the Resurrection.
- Make and/or fill an Easter basket to give to a shut-in.

❏ Signature

Jesus and his apostles were on
a mountain.

He said,
  "Go and baptize all people.
  Teach them everything I told you.
  I am with you always.
  I will send my Spirit."

Jesus returned to his Father.

His friends no longer saw him.

The apostles went back to the city.

They prayed for the Holy Spirit to come.

The apostles waited and prayed.

Mother Mary was with them.

They heard a strong wind.

They saw tongues of fire.

They knew God was there.

Jesus kept his promise.

He sent his Spirit.

Mary and the apostles were filled with the Holy Spirit.

Color the tongues of fire red.

The Holy Spirit is God.

He filled the apostles' hearts with love.

He helped the apostles to become
God's new family, the Church.

The Holy Spirit made the apostles
loving and brave.

They had strength to go out and tell
people about Jesus' great love.

The Holy Spirit is with us too.

He helps us to show everyone that
Jesus loves us all.

Use the clues to work this puzzle.

Across

2. It was above the head of Mary and each apostle.

3. The Holy Spirit put it in the hearts of the apostles.

Down

1. The apostles felt this way after the Holy Spirit came.

We Remember

Who is the Holy Spirit?

The Holy Spirit is God.
He is Jesus' Spirit.

We Respond

Come Holy Spirit!
Fill my heart with Jesus' love.

God's big Christian family is called the Church.

All baptized people belong to it.

Jesus' Spirit is with the Church.

The Holy Spirit helps Christians bring Jesus' love to the world.

Before Jesus went to heaven, he spoke
to Peter.

He said, "Simon, do you love me?"

Peter said, "Yes, Lord, you know that I
love you."

Jesus said,

"Feed my sheep."
adapted from John 21:17

Jesus told Peter to care for his family,
the Church.

Then he made Peter the leader of
the Church.

Peter was the first **pope.**

The Church has a pope today too.

He acts for Jesus on earth.

We call him the Holy Father.

He and the other bishops lead

Catholics in spreading Jesus' love.

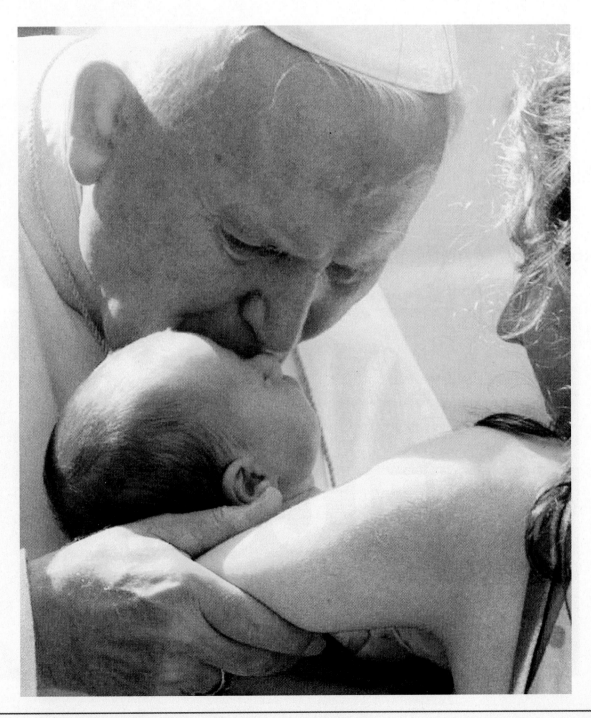

The one who baptized you said,
  "[Your name], I baptize you
  in the name of the Father,
  and of the Son,
  and of the Holy Spirit."

We joined the Catholic Church
when we were baptized.

We became Catholics.

The Catholic Christian family
welcomed us into the Church.

Jesus invites all people to belong
to his Church.

Color the word on the banner.

Draw yourself at Mass with God's people, the Church.

I belong to the holy Catholic Church.

We Remember

To what Church do you belong?

I belong to the Catholic Church.
I am a Catholic.

Words to Know

pope   Catholics

We Respond

Lord Jesus, help me to be a good Catholic Christian.

FAMILY CORNER

The continuing reality of Christ's presence in the world today is expressed through his Church, the means he has chosen to unite our human family with himself. Christians who realize that Jesus is among them warmly welcome everyone into their lives.

Read
John 21:15–17

Discuss
- how the lives of Catholics should set them apart from nonbelievers
- God's goodness in giving his Church a leader to care for his people
- how refusing to let your children do everything they want means that you love them

Pray
May all be one in Christ!

Do
- Invite someone to church with you.
- Participate in a parish activity.
- Start a scrapbook about Church news.
- Read and talk about the present Holy Father or previous popes.
- Name as many people as you can who help your parish family.
- Talk about our Christian family ancestors, the saints, and how they lived their lives as Catholic Christians.

❏ Signature

129

Jesus gave us his mother to be our mother too.

Mary is the Mother of the Church.

She always listened to God.

We call her our Blessed Mother.

One day Jesus took Mary, body and soul, to heaven.

He made her queen.

Now Mary prays for us and helps us to be like Jesus.

We pray to Mary and honor her.

We try to be kind and loving as she is.

Someday Jesus will take us to heaven if we follow him.

We will live forever with Jesus, Mary, the saints, and angels.

Draw yourself taking flowers to Mary.

Immaculate Mary,
Your praises we sing.
You reign now with Christ,
Our Redeemer and King.

Ave, ave, ave Maria!
Ave, ave, Maria!

Draw yourself taking flowers to Mary.

Connect the dots to make a gift for Mary.
Color the gift.

Mary, Queen of Heaven!

We Remember

Who is Mary?
Mary is God's Mother and our mother and queen.

We Respond

O my Queen, O my Mother, I love you and give myself to you.

FAMILY CORNER

Christ, as he was dying on the cross, gave us his mother, Mary, to be our mother. Mary shows us how to be a Christian by her response to God during her life. She is the Mother of the Church and the model for followers of Jesus.

Read
John 19:25–27

Discuss
• how gifts are a sign of love
• how good God is to give us our heavenly mother and the times in our lives when she gives us special care
• the things Mary did that show us how to be good Christians

Pray
Holy Mary, Mother of God, pray for us!

Do
• Make a May altar in your home and plan when you will get together as a family to honor Mary.
• Participate in your parish celebration honoring Mary.
• Tell what you can remember about Mary. Take turns sharing what you know.

❏ Signature

The Holy Spirit helped the apostles teach people about Jesus.

He helped men write the Gospels of Matthew, Mark, Luke, and John.

The **Gospels** are a part of the Bible.

They tell the Good News that Jesus loves and saved us.

The Holy Spirit helps us listen to the Gospel at Mass.

He helps us listen when the priest tells us about Jesus.

Then the Holy Spirit helps us to be like Jesus.

Long ago the Holy Spirit helped the Church.

He helped the first Christians to love God and others.

He helped them to pray and share.

The Holy Spirit helps us today
to be good Christians.

He helps us to love God and others.

He helps us to pray and share.

People should say of us, "See how these Catholics
love one another."

Love is the badge of a Catholic.

Trace the words on the badge.

Light shines.

Once Jesus said,

> "You are the light of the world."
> Matthew 5:14

Jesus wants us to let God's goodness shine out from us.

The Holy Spirit helps us to spread the Good News of Jesus.

We can help people we meet to know Jesus.

We can help people in mission lands to know Jesus.

We can pray that many will join God's family, the Church.

Draw rays of light from the pictures to show that you want your light to shine.

Draw yourself bringing someone Jesus' love.
Write the person's name on the line.

I can bring Jesus' love to _____ .

Write the Good News about Jesus.

_____

_____

_____

_____

_____

_____

We Remember

Who helps us to spread the Good News of Jesus' love?

The Holy Spirit helps us to spread the Good News of Jesus' love.

Word to Know

Gospel

We Respond

Holy Spirit, help me to spread Jesus' love.

FAMILY CORNER

The Gospels tell us how much God loves us and how our loving words and deeds show that his Spirit is with us.

Read
Matthew 5:14–16

Discuss
• specific ways each one in your family has brightened the lives of others
• a specific missionary for whom your family will pray and sacrifice

Pray
Lord, may all our good works give you praise!

Do
• Read a Bible story at bedtime and discuss the events of the day in its light.
• Send a note to a relative, friend, or neighbor about the Good News.
• Tell the story of a modern missionary.
• Pray that those God is calling to the priesthood, diaconate, or religious life may answer his call.
• Begin memorizing favorite Bible verses.

❏ Signature _____

137

Heaven and earth are full of your glory.

Our world can be very beautiful.

All the beautiful and good things in it give glory to God.

The Holy Spirit is always at work in the world.

He helps everything to give glory to God.

The Holy Spirit helps us to give
glory to God.

We praise the three Persons in God
when we pray.

Glory to the Father,
and to the Son,
and to the Holy Spirit.
As it was in the beginning,
is now,
and will be for ever.
                    Amen.

Kind words give glory to God.

Write the missing letters to complete the words.

"May I __h_____?"   "I __l_____ you."

"Come and __p_____."   "I am __s_____."

Good actions give glory to God.

We give glory to God when we obey him,
our parents, and others.

We give glory to God when we help others.

We give glory to God when we sing, laugh,
and play.

We give glory to God when we help make
our world good and beautiful.

Draw a picture of yourself giving glory to God.

I can give glory to God.

Jesus said he would be with us always.

Jesus is with us in his Holy Spirit.

He will be with us this summer.

We can help others know that

We can help our world to give glory to God.

Outline the letters.

Then color or design the words.

Color the boxes, using the code, to see what comes when we give God glory.

J	J	J	J	J	J	J	J	J	J	J	J	J	J	J	J	J	J	J
J	E	E	E	E	E	S	S	S	S	S	U	U	U	U	U	U	U	J
J	E	E	E	S	E	S	J	J	S	U	E	U	U	U	E	U	J	
J	E	E	E	S	E	S	J	S	J	S	U	U	E	U	E	U	U	J
J	E	E	E	S	E	S	J	S	J	S	U	U	U	E	U	U	U	J
J	E	S	E	S	E	S	J	S	J	S	U	U	U	E	U	U	U	J
J	E	S	S	E	S	J	J	J	S	U	U	U	E	U	U	U	J	
J	E	E	E	E	S	S	S	S	S	U	U	U	U	U	U	U	J	
J	J	J	J	J	J	J	J	J	J	J	J	J	J	J	J	J	J	J

Code

J blue
E red
S yellow
U green

We Remember

Why do we give glory to God?
We give glory to God because he is good and he made us.

We Respond

Glory to the Father, and to the Son, and to the Holy Spirit.

FAMILY CORNER

We give glory to a person when we praise and honor him or her for accomplishing a great deed. We give glory to God when we pray and when our words and actions reflect his goodness. God has invited us to enter into his glory and to share it with everyone.

 Read
Matthew 25:31–40

Discuss

- the daily opportunities you can use to do good things and give glory to God
- the kind words and deeds that made you happy today
- what your family does that shows your relatives and neighbors that God is good

 Pray
Glory to the Father, and to the Son, and to the Holy Spirit!

Do

- Read or relate episodes from the lives of the saints.
- Pray for people whose needs are made known in the daily news.
- Think of someone or something beginning with each letter of the alphabet that gives glory to God. Tell how each one praises God or reflects his goodness.
- Make a family vacation calendar. In the box for each day print something you want to do to grow in love.
- Help your child keep a "God Is Good" diary, with a sentence or picture telling about something beautiful he or she saw or did that day.
- Look back over the Do's in other chapters and plan how your family can grow together in faith during the summer.

_____

❏ Signature

143

The Christian Family Album

Priest
Christians
Pope
Mary
Peter Luke Matthew Mark John
Jesus
Holy Spirit
Sister
Apostles

The Church is God's big, loving Christian family.

Some of God's family are already with him in heaven.

Tell something about each picture in the Christian Family Album.

FAMILY FEATURE

A Family Missionary

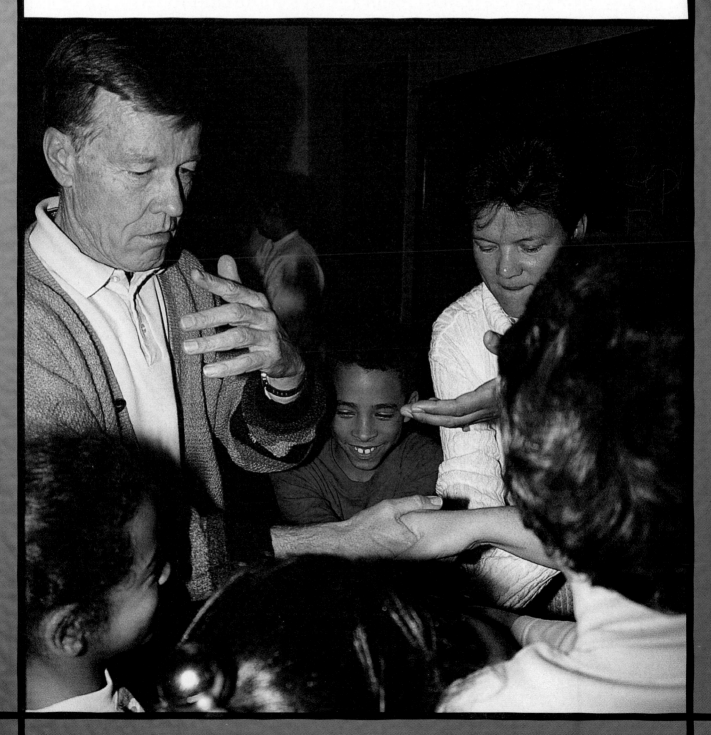

Father Don Bosco is a Carmelite priest from India who works as a missionary in the United States. Missionaries are working in countries all over the world to fulfill Christ's command to tell the Good News of God's love to all nations. They show God's love to people by helping them improve their lives. We have all been baptized into Jesus Christ and took on his mission to spread the Good News. Although most of us can't be physically present in another country to do this, we can support those who are.

The Cahill family has adopted Father Don Bosco, whom they met on a trip. They write to him, pray for him at their family prayers, and read about any area in which he is working. They send him money and things that help with his work. For instance, when the *Catechism of the Catholic Church* was published, the family bought Father a copy. The Cahill children, Karen and Bob, save part of their allowance for Father. At Christmas and Easter the family remembers him and his work in a special way.

Your family might like to adopt a missionary in order to be more directly involved with the mission work of the Church. There might be someone in your parish or diocese who is a missionary and who would appreciate your support. You might contact a mission organization and ask for the name of a missionary. In addition to foreign missions, there are home missions that work in their own countries.

Addresses of some mission organizations are listed here. Many religious communities do missionary work also.

Society for the
Propagation of the Faith
366 Fifth Avenue
New York, NY 10001

Comboni Missionaries
8108 Beechmont Avenue
Cincinnati, OH 45230

Society of St. Columban
P.O. Box 10
St. Columbans, NE 68056

Maryknoll
Maryknoll, NY 10545

Glenmary Home Missioners
P.O. Box 465618
Cincinnati, OH 45246

The Story of Jesus

Number the stories about the
Good News of Jesus in order.

SUPPLEMENT

Sharing Advent as a Family
Celebration of the Feast of Saint Nicholas, December 6

Tell the story of good St. Nicholas. Then decide how everyone in your family can be like him in bringing joy to others during Advent by performing secret deeds of kindness.

The Story of St. Nicholas

A long time ago, in a time we call the fourth century, in a place named Asia Minor, there lived a good and kind bishop. His name was Nicholas. Because he loved God and others so much and now lives with God in heaven, we call him Saint Nicholas. If you say the name St. Nicholas very, very quickly you will hear that it sounds somewhat like "Santa Claus."

St. Nicholas gave so many gifts to others that when people found a nice surprise they would just go to Nicholas and thank him. They thought he must have left the present. Children were special friends of St. Nicholas. Some people believe that he still brings them gifts today. On his feast day, December 6, he is said to leave candy or nuts or other surprises in children's shoes or stockings.

The story of St. Nicholas spread to many faraway places. Pictures of St. Nicholas often show him with a huge bag full of good things he is going to give to others, riding along in a sleigh pulled by reindeer. A long time ago in the Far North, where there are many reindeer and a great deal of ice and snow, people often used to travel by sleigh. People up there thought St. Nicholas did too. Everyone liked to be around St. Nicholas because he was so good and kind.

Preparing Manger Gifts

Talk about how Joseph prepared the manger, arranging the straw to make a comfortable bed for Jesus the night he was born. Make a manger or a cradle in which the children may place something soft, such as a piece of yellow yarn, whenever they are kind or thoughtful. By Christmas morning the expressions of love will have made the hard bed into a soft crib.

A Birthday Celebration

On Christmas have a real birthday celebration with cake and with gifts for Jesus. The gifts to Jesus could be drawings showing the loving acts that have prepared each one's heart to live fully in God's love. Let everyone place a candle in the cake as a symbol of good deeds that keep the light of Christ shining in the world.

Blessing of the Christmas Tree

Gather around your family tree and pray.

Leader: All the earth has seen the saving power of God.

All: Joy to the world, the Lord has come.

Leader: The Lord has made his salvation known.

All: Let earth receive her king.

Leader: Let us pray.

All: Almighty Father, we ask you to bless this tree that we have decorated as a sign and reminder that the coming of your Son brought light and joy to the world. Help us to be bright lights bringing joy to others. We ask this through Jesus, your Son. Amen.

(*Song*) "Joy to the World"

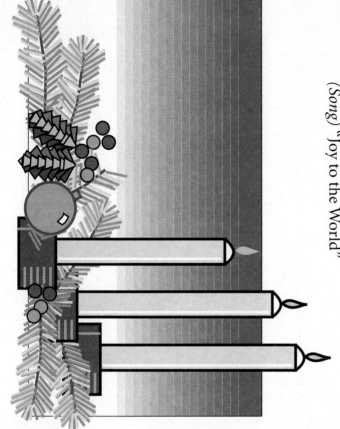

Family Prayers for the Advent Season

Our hearts desire the warmth of your love, O God.

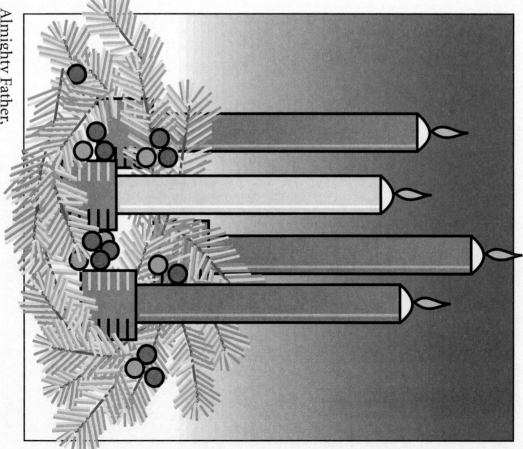

Almighty Father,
give us the joy of your love
to prepare the way for Christ our Lord.
Help us to serve you and one another.
We ask this through our Lord Jesus Christ, your Son.

Everyone in the family can be involved in making an Advent wreath for your home. Explain the symbolism of each part. Decide how each person will participate in preparing the wreath and in daily or weekly family devotions. The first time you gather to pray around the wreath, have someone review the meaning of each part.

Circular Shape

The Advent wreath is a circle. We cannot find the end or the beginning of a circle. The circular Advent wreath reminds us that Jesus came to give us a life that will never end, eternal life with God in heaven.

Evergreen Branches

The evergreen branches used to make the circle do not change color as do the leaves on other kinds of trees. The evergreens in the Advent wreath remind us that God never changes: God always has loved us and always will.

Candles

There are four candles on the Advent wreath, one for each week in Advent. They remind us that the Jewish people waited a long time for the Savior to come. The burning candles remind us that Christ, the Light of the World, brightens the darkness around us. Each week we light one more candle, a sign that the more we let Christ into our lives, the brighter our lives will be.

Opening Prayer

O God, bless this Advent wreath. May it help us prepare to welcome Jesus, your Son, into our lives, letting the light of his love shine through us. Amen.

Week 1   *(Light 1 candle.)* Come to us, Lord Jesus. Warm our hearts with your love. Help us to prepare for your coming. Help us to see the good things we can do. Help us to see the good things others do. Come, Lord Jesus! *(Pause for silent prayer.)*

Week 2   *(Light 2 candles.)* We believe in you, Lord. We know that you can help us to love each other more. You are our light. Come, Lord Jesus! *(Pause for silent prayer.)*

Week 3   *(Light 3 candles.)* Jesus, we want your coming to make a difference in how we live and love. Open our hearts to hear you telling us how we can bring peace and joy to others. Come, Lord Jesus! *(Pause for silent prayer.)*

Week 4   *(Light 4 candles.)* Quiet the worries and fears in our hearts, Lord. Give us your peace. Thank you for the life you share with us. Help us to share that life with others. Come, Lord Jesus! *(Pause for silent prayer.)*

A Time to Grow and Change

During Lent we get ready for Easter.

We try to do more things that show we love God and others.

Trace around the dotted lines and see the surprise.

Color the surprise.

The caterpillar has a new life.

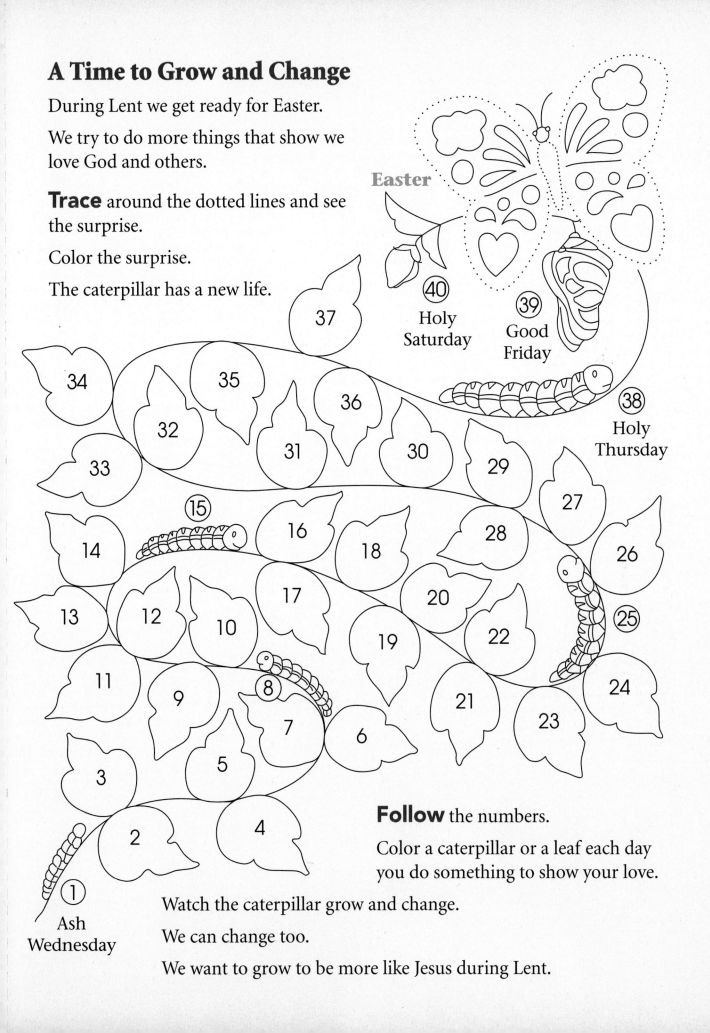

Easter

40 Holy Saturday

39 Good Friday

38 Holy Thursday

37

34 35 36 32 31 30 29 27 28 26 33 15 16 18 20 25 14 17 19 22 24 13 12 10 8 21 23 11 9 7 6 5 4 3 2

1 Ash Wednesday

Follow the numbers.

Color a caterpillar or a leaf each day you do something to show your love.

Watch the caterpillar grow and change.

We can change too.

We want to grow to be more like Jesus during Lent.

Jesus, you rose from the dead on Easter Sunday.

† You gave God's life to us.

Thank you, Jesus!

The Way of the Cross

Jesus, I want to follow you on the Way of the Cross.

I want to thank you for loving me so much.

A

13 Jesus Is Taken Down

Mary held Jesus in her arms.

† Mary, help me to love Jesus as you love him.

2 Jesus Takes His Cross

Jesus took the heavy cross with love.

† Jesus, help me to do hard things with love.

1 Jesus Must Die

Some of the people wanted Jesus to die.

† Jesus, you were willing to die for us.

Thank you, Jesus.

14 Jesus Is Buried

The friends of Jesus put him in the tomb.

† Jesus, you died to save us.

You rose to bring us new life.

3 Jesus Falls

The cross made Jesus fall.

† Jesus, it was hard to carry the cross.

You carried it to save us from sin.

12 Jesus Died on the Cross

After three hours, Jesus died on the cross.

† Jesus, you died so we can live with God in heaven.

Thank you for loving us so much.

11 Jesus Is Nailed to the Cross

Jesus forgave the men who
hurt him.

He prayed,
   "Father, forgive them."

† Jesus, teach me to forgive
   others who hurt me.

4 Jesus Meets His Mother

Mary was sad to see Jesus suffer.

She knew he must die for her
and for us.

† Thank you, Mary, for being
   the Mother of our Savior.

B

9 Jesus Falls Again

Jesus fell again under his cross.

He was very tired, but he did
not stop.

† Jesus, help me to keep on
   trying to be good.

6 Veronica Helps Jesus

Veronica was sorry for Jesus.

She wiped his face.

† Jesus, help me to be kind as
   Veronica was.

5 Simon Helps Jesus

Jesus found it hard to carry the heavy cross by himself.

Simon helped him.

† Jesus, show me how to help others.

10 Jesus' Clothes Are Taken Away

The soldiers took away Jesus' clothes.

They hurt him.

† Jesus, you suffered for us.

Thank you.

7 Jesus Falls the Second Time

Jesus fell a second time.

He got up and carried the cross again.

† Thank you, Jesus, for carrying your cross for us.

8 The Women Are Sorry for Jesus

Some women cried to see Jesus suffer.

He spoke to them.

† Jesus, teach me to care when others suffer and to help them.

Trust in the LORD and do good.

Psalm 37:3

Daniel was a leader in his country. The other leaders were jealous. They said to the king, "Make a law that no one may pray for thirty days. Anyone who prays will be thrown to the lions." The king made the law.

Daniel loved God, so he still prayed three times a day. The king liked Daniel, but he could not change his law. Daniel was thrown into a den of lions.

The next morning the king went to the den. There was Daniel. He was unhurt because he trusted in God.

adapted from Daniel 6:2-29

12

I love Jesus

Jesus loves me

Name _____

Song-Prayers

You are great, and you do wondrous deeds.
Teach me, O LORD, your way.

adapted from Psalm 86:10–11

LORD, you know me.
You know everything I do.
You know how I think.
You put your hand upon me.
You are everywhere!

adapted from Psalm 139:1–5

I am sad.
Have you forgotten me, God?
Why are you so sad, my soul?
Hope in God.
I shall again thank God!

adapted from Psalm 42:10–12

11

Color a prayer bead every time you use this book about the Bible.

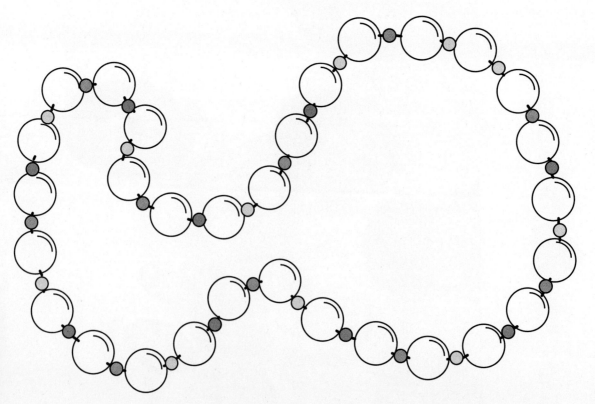

2

You will come to me, Jesus.

Take and eat.
Matthew 26:26

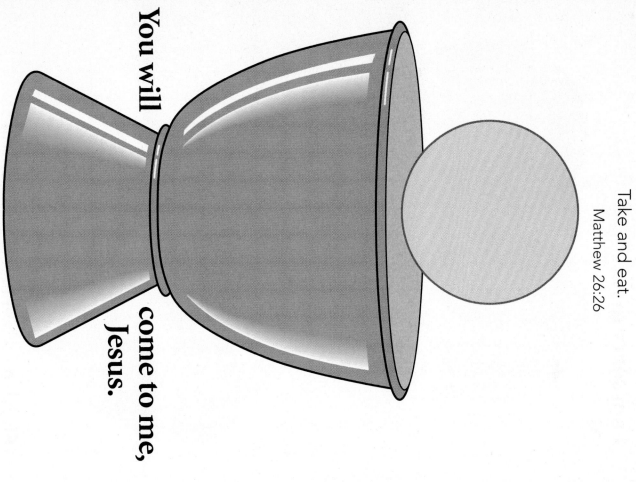

Christ died for us.
Romans 5:8

Help me.

You died for me.

Love me.

Watch over me.

Jesus

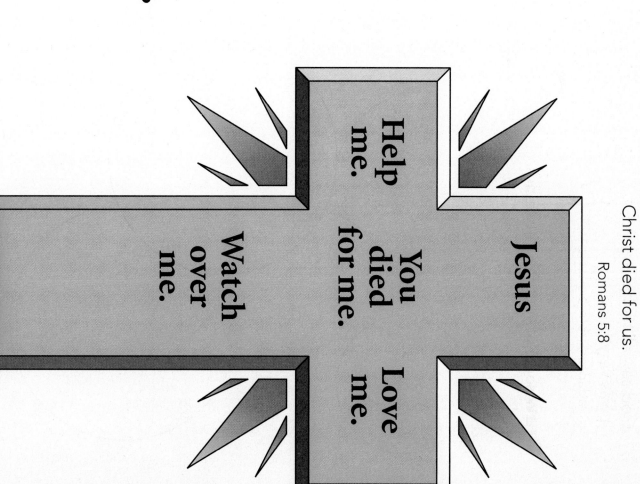

I am sorry for . . .

Finish the prayer in your own words in your heart.

God saw all he had made.
It was very good.
adapted from Genesis 1:31

Draw some of your favorite things.

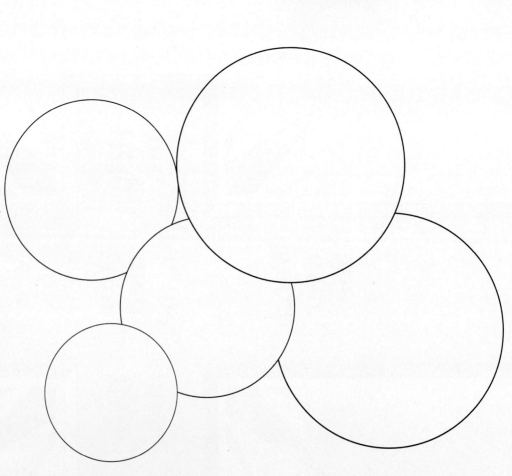

God looks for us.

Jesus told this story.

A woman had ten coins.

She lost one.

She lighted a lamp and swept the floor.

When she found the coin, she called her friends together.

She said, "Rejoice with me. I found my coin."

adapted from Luke 15:8-10

When we go away from God, God wants us back.

Jesus, help me to be like you.

Jesus teaches people that God loves them.

Jesus helps the sick.

Jesus gives food to the hungry.

Mary, show me how to love God.

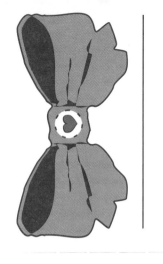

I will help.

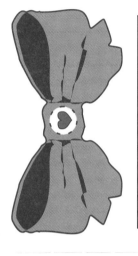

I will help.

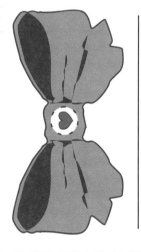

I will help.

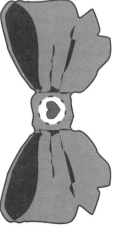

I will help.

VIP
You are a very important person.

VIP
You are a very important person.

VIP
You are a very important person.

VIP
You are a very important person.

Puzzle: Chapter 14

Card: Supplement, Chapter 1 ⇩

© Loyola Press

Angel sent by God
to guide me,

be my light and
walk beside me.

Be my guardian
and protect me.

On the paths of life
direct me.

O, Jesus, I offer you
all I think, do, and say.

Bless me and make me
like you today.

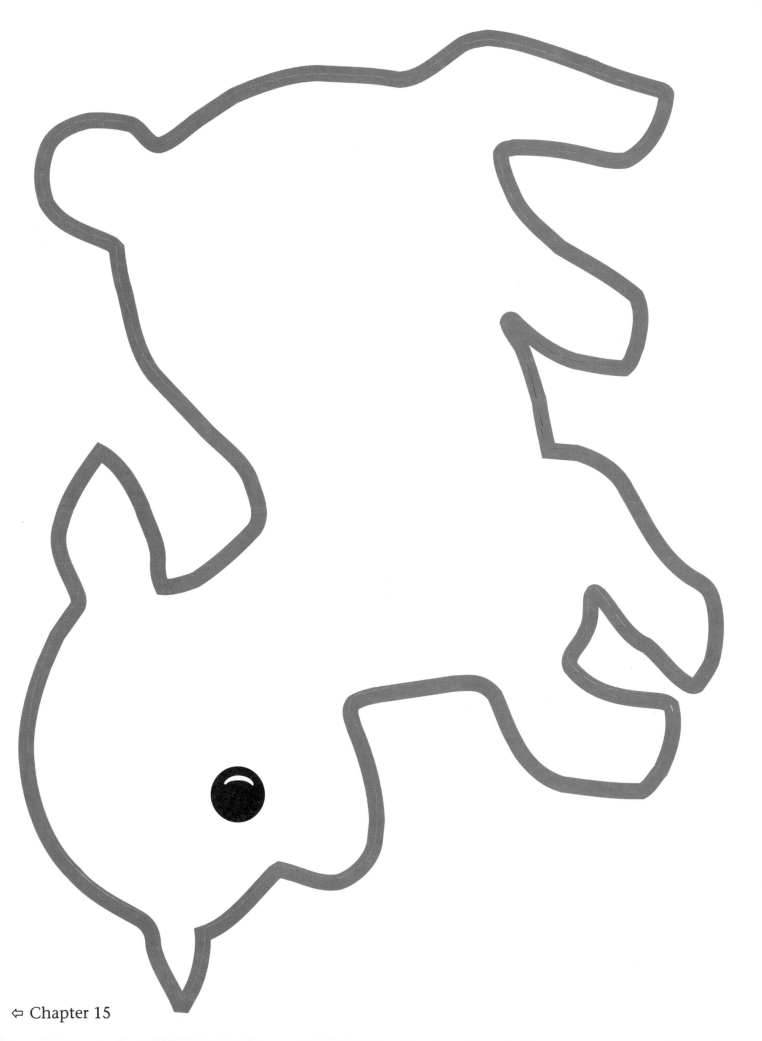

Chapter 18

© Loyola Press

Chapter 10

Chapter 11

Fold front

Fold back

Fold front

Join strips at end notches to
form rings for bases.

Insert figures in side
notches to stand.

Chapter 13

Chapter 19

I am with you.

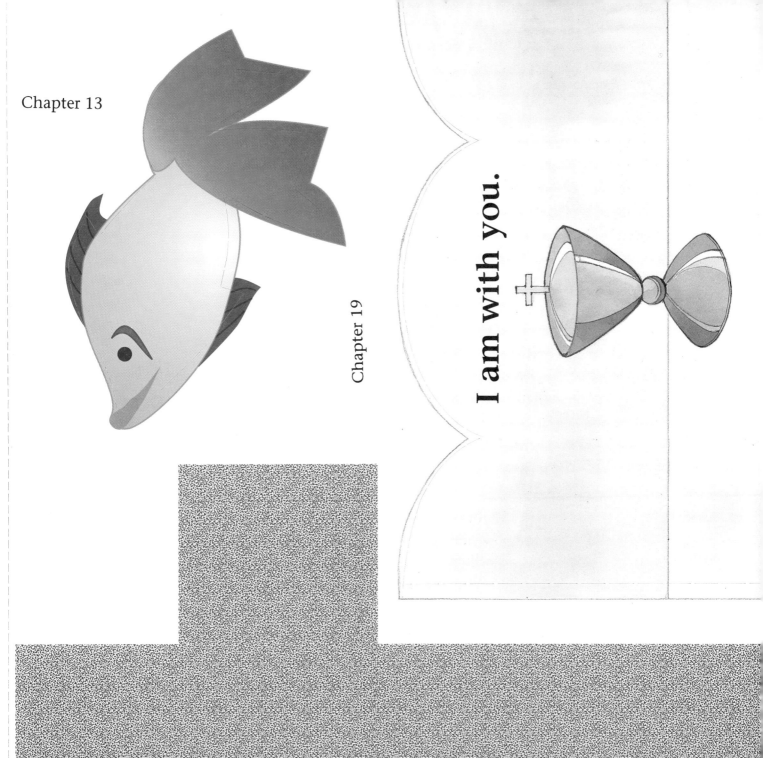

Chapter 1

Bless us, O Lord,
and these your gifts.

Lord, every morning I pray to you,
and at night I come before you.

adapted from Psalm 5:3; 77:3

Fold

Fold

Chapter 7

JOY

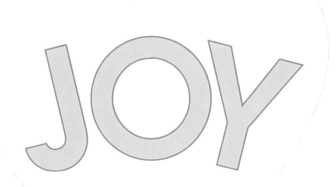

God is my Father.

Glory to God

Chapter 1

© Loyola Press

Chapter 9

© Loyola Press

Chapter 3

© Loyola Press

Chapter 20

© Loyola Press

Chapter 5

© Loyola Press

Chapter 10

© Loyola Press

Chapter 23

© Loyola Press

Chapter 25

© Loyola Press